LONGMAN TUT(

GW01091116

The Tutor
and the
Tutor Group

Developing your role as a Tutor

Michael Marland CBE MA

Headteacher, North Westminster Community School
Honorary Professor of Education, Warwick University

Longman Group UK Limited,
Longman House, Burnt Mill, Harlow,
Essex CM20 2JE, England
and Associated Companies throughout the world.

First published 1989
Second impression 1990

Set in 11/13 pt Baskerville
Produced by Longman Group (FE) Ltd
Printed in Malaysia
by Polygraphic Marketing Sdn. Bhd.,
Balakong, Selangor Darul Ehsan

ISBN 0 582 20688 X

*'A Tutor is a teacher
whose subject is
the pupil herself.'*

Contents

Preface

Pastoral care has a long and vigorous tradition in our schools. Recently this has been heightened by the contractual requirements of conditions of service (see Appendix A), the growth of the National Association for Pastoral Care in Education, and encouragement for personal and social education and pastoral care from central government and HMI:

> Personal and social development and responsibility are intrinsic to the nature of education. It is something from which no teacher can opt out.
>
> (HMI, 1989, p. 1)

The main 'delivery', that impersonal sounding but effective term, for pastoral care is the Tutor responsible for a Tutor Group. Indeed, most secondary teachers have tutorial responsibilities, but very many consider themselves under-prepared (see pages 8–12). This small book is designed as a practical guide to the aims and methods of tutoring in a secondary school. I hope that it will be found helpful not only by new Tutors, but also by those very many conscientious, caring, and hard-working experienced Tutors who would like to reflect on their work and develop it.

Really, to write a text on tutoring is to write an analysis of secondary education: the Tutor's role is genuinely, and not merely theoretically, 'central', and her task in supporting learning and acting as the 'consolidator' (the DES phrase,

DES, 1988, p. 2) of 'cross-curricular themes', in particular Personal, Social, and Health Education ('PSE' or 'PHSE'), takes the Tutor's concerns into all aspects of the curriculum and their inter-relationship. However, I have endeavoured to restrict the focus of this book to the work of the Tutor, and this does not pretend to be a general study of pastoral care or of the whole-school responsibility for personal and social education.

Although this book for Tutors on tutoring is written as part of the Longman Tutorial Resources series, and therefore relates especially to the material for a tutorial programme devised in six books for that series, it is planned to stand on its own. The arguments and methods are, I suggest, generally applicable in secondary schools. Many of the examples chosen come from LTR, as those pupil books were devised for this approach.

Very many conscientious, thoughtful, and sensitive teachers are developing their tutoring skills in schools throughout the country, despite little or no initial training and in some cases despite limited support. It is also clear that there are some schools where it is difficult to encourage good tutoring and also schools where keen teachers do not find the guidelines and leadership they need. Generally, though, pastoral care and tutoring are becoming more systematic, professional, and energetic. I hope that this small study, which endeavours to bring together a range of recent research with the realities and practicalities of daily life for a Tutor, will be of some help to those many Tutors wanting to enrich and extend their work.

Michael Marland

Acknowledgements

I should like to thank the members of the National Association for Pastoral Care in Education, from whom I have learned so much at annual conferences, many local meetings, and from its excellent journal *Pastoral Care*. I should also like to thank that small group of thinkers and writers on pastoral care, whose books are listed on pages 155–65, who have advanced the work. Especially, I should like to thank the Tutors and tutees of North Westminster School, from whom I have learned so much.

I am grateful to Stella Fleuri for her efficient word-processing.

Finally, I am grateful to the following for permission to use extracts and examples from their work: Anna Dolezal, Linda Marsh, and Chris Watkins for the examples from their Longman Tutorial Resources books; Frank Monaghan for the work sheet he devised used on page 54; Ann Irving for the extract from her book *Study and Information Skills Across the Curriculum* reproduced on page 59; Professor Carol Dweck for the data reproduced on page 25; Adam Weinbren for the worksheet he devised used on page 39; and North Westminster School for the examples reproduced on pages 29 and 102.

Index compiled by Peva Keane.
Photograph on page 87 by Sally and Richard Greenhill.

M. M.

1 The idea of a Tutor

The central task of the Tutor

From one point of view education is a process in all its many aspects of enabling a child to become a student and then more fully a person. This is the major task of the Tutor's charge of being responsible for 'personal, educational, and vocational guidance'.

Indeed, at the heart of pastoral care is the task which the psychologist Erik H. Erikson calls 'the crisis of identity'. He defines the central adolescent task as answering the question: 'What do I want to make of myself and what do I have to work with?' (Erikson, 1971, p. 314) The pastoral task is to enable the tutee to develop her or his exploration of those questions in terms ranging from relationships with peers in class to society more generally, and encouraging self-understanding.

The Tutor's main aim, then, is to help the tutee decide who she is, how she wants to be, and how she can change her behaviour in whatever aspects she wishes. This is 'personal guidance'.

If the tutee is to be able to achieve this, she or he must be able to make for her- or himself best use of the school, to 'exploit' it, if you like. To be a successful student, the child has to learn how to be a pupil – a huge and complex learning task. This is the Tutor's role of 'educational guidance'.

It is clear that success at school has a range of effects on the young person's 'pathways from childhood to adult life' (the powerful phrase is Professor Rutter's). Not only does the more frequently discussed examination portfolio open up or close down certain paths, and therefore certain occupations, milieu, and income levels, success or failure to take a grip on school can influence a person's ability to cope in the future:

> There is evidence that successful coping and/or positive experiences tend to be protective, and it is possible that the protection lies in the enhanced self-confidence that derives from the experiences.
>
> (Rutter, 1989, p. 43)

One of the daunting aspects of responsibility for pastoral care is the research confirmation that success at school positively affects mosts aspects of later life. In the case of institution-reared girls, for instance:

> Positive school experiences were associated with an increased tendency to exert 'planning' in relation to both marriage and careers. It is suggested that this was because the successful coping in one situation – school – increased the likelihood that the girls would feel in control of other aspects of their lives and able to do something about the situation.
>
> (Rutter, 1989, pp. 43–4)

Every teacher and every aspect of the environment and procedures of a school should be calculated to offer the possibility of positive, successful coping and the building of appropriate self-esteem. It is the Tutor's special responsibility: through the Tutor's guidance the growing student is better able to make school cohere, and to find a node of success. If there were no Tutors in a school there would be no 'home' for a pupil to go to when he or she needed it. The

Tutor's offer of 'home' is, though, no mere soft cushion: a home at its best demands, enables growth, stimulates, encourages self-esteem, develops judgement, and creates a sense of coherence.

A pupil needs to feel 'safe' in the wider community of the school; this of course includes the physical, and even petty bullying and racial or sexual harassment are clearly very distressing, having effects beyond the incidents themselves. More than that, though, all pupils needs to feel psychologically comfortable – able to be themselves without being totally pulled into the peer group's ways or being ostracised. The Tutor contributes to meeting this need in two complementary ways: firstly, by the development of the tutee's appropriate assertiveness and inter-personal skills through the tutorial programme; secondly, by creating in the tutor room and in the Tutor Group a mutually supportive atmosphere: 'Sir, do you know what happened to Ramesh today?' The Tutor should encourage the end-of-the day bringing back of the pleasures and difficulties of the day. Of course, the problem is that this ideal is difficult for all teachers to offer, and for all pupils to accept. I have often gleaned from newly trained teachers that their B.Ed. or PGCE has given them a vivid, over-arching vision of the aim of their *subject* in schooling, but that they have frequently felt unconfident and a little vague about the possible steps needed to bring that vision to their pupils. Conversely, having had virtually no academic introduction to pastoral care, the concept of 'being a Tutor' is built up from the snatches of advice, administrative instructions, and fleeting briefings from keen teachers on the job in such a way that tutoring is seen as a mass of detailed tasks, lacking coherence or point beyond the immediate administration. Lacking an over-arching vision and bombarded with urgent demands to complete tasks, the Tutor becomes an overloaded functionary, reeling from 'problems' and rarely in a position to look ahead. Like so many year heads, Tutors are then forced to be reactive and not proactive; 'pastoral care' equates with 'coping with problems', and the major needs of the tutees cannot be met in the welter of effort to cope with their demands.

Pastoral care can never be successful unless it pulls itself above this responding to what has gone wrong and looks ahead, using the group and group-study material and activities to help the individual understand herself better. It is also about helping young people look to the future, both immediate and distant, and to take control of their inner, their social, and their learning lives. This involves making sense of, but being independent of, social and peer-group pressures.

This target of personal growth is, obviously, a central aim of the whole-school curriculum, but the Tutor is the special exponent. The Tutor's narrower, specific responsibilities, such as home/school liaison, welfare support, individual counselling, and discipline, are only parts of the Tutor's role and must always be interpreted in the light of the larger task: the sum of the details will not necessarily create the required whole. Busy application to a myriad of tasks can obscure the guidance role. Each needs seeing and meeting in the light of the overall task, and that also needs embodying in specially planned whole-group work.

Difficult as the task of tutoring is (and the next section discusses those difficulties and some ways of coping), the key to success is to have a firm vision of the *idea* of a Tutor and to exploit the tasks to serve this vision.

The difficulties of tutoring

A teacher brings to the pupils a range of skills, knowledge, understanding of concepts, and attitudes. Some of these have been systematically learned and the teacher's grasp of them is conscious and can be coherently articulated. Thus a physics teacher's scientific knowledge or a French teacher's understanding of the French language are the result of clearly focused study. However, other aspects of a teacher's abilities have been far less consciously learned and are far less coherently expressible: our way of analysing problems, our views on the use of time, our 'teaching' about ways of relating to each other, . . . These, and many more aspects of our 'teaching', are erratic, intangible, and less available for scrutiny, and thus criticism or support. The central reason why tutoring is difficult is that the Tutor's main contribution is culled from those less defined aspects of his professional concerns.

Of the 'subject', the Tutor brings no systematic background study and little more specific knowledge than that potentially possessed by the pupil. It is this removing of a strong expertise, such as the physical education teacher or the history teacher has, that can lead the Tutor to feel lost.

A further fundamental pedagogical difficulty grows out of the central aim of pastoral care: if it is about helping the individual understand herself, how can the Tutor find time and space to work with all these individuals? Most Tutors often feel a frantic wish to send all but one tutee away.

Elsewhere, I have defined the art of pastoral care as to 'help individuals without giving individual help' (Marland, 1983, p. 26). The individuals who are in the group should be in the forefront of the Tutor's ambitions, but it is the *group* that will normally have to be the vehicle for helping those individuals. This is partly for the negative reason that there will never be more than a very small amount of time for each individual, but also for the much more positive reason that the group of people is a good medium for learning about people! The other members are not, as they sometimes appear, in, say, an art or mathematics lesson, 'in the way' between the pupil and the teacher: the other tutees and the individual's reaction to them is part of the learning material. Indeed, a well-mobilised group (as is discussed in Chapter 3) is also part of the teaching: there is a sense in which the Tutor's task is to enable the group to tutor itself.

A further difficulty is an iatrogenic one – that is a disease caused by the physicians! Although many schools speak of the importance of tutoring, and some heads speak of the Tutor as 'the heart of the school', many schools find it difficult to make the physical and organisational support of tutoring easy. For instance:

- The requirement of being a Tutor is not included in the advertisements.
- Similarly, it is often not in the job specification.
- Frequently it is not covered in the interview.
- There is a poor or non-existent job description.
- There is little opportunity to be briefed by the team leader.
- There are few or no team meetings.
- Material for tutorial sessions is skimpy – or there may be none.
- Tutorial material storage is inadequate.
- There are inadequate clerical, reception, and communication facilities.
- There is too little time for tutorial sessions.

Indeed, more generally, pastoral care is undervalued in a number of schools.

In well-run schools middle-management pastoral team leaders will give detailed briefings and help by observing tutor period sessions, swapping good ideas, and giving detailed observation notes. There should be tutor-planning and discussion meetings under the leadership of these team leaders, which are also excellent times to pick up tips from others so that each member of the team pools her or his problems and successes and gains from other team members.

However, not all schools have managed to create a clear structure of support for Tutors. For instance, in a generally praising inspection report of a small school with a strongly caring ethos, the LEA team wrote:

> The heads of year each oversee a team of form mistresses who are the first point of reference for matters of lateness, attendance and difficult behaviour. In turn, the heads of year used to be accountable to the deputy head though now it is the senior who chairs their meetings. There seems to be some confusion amongst teachers concerning senior management role definition and lines of accountability in this respect.
>
> Whilst the heads of year have overall pastoral and academic responsibility for the girls in their year it is apparent that their involvement in the overview of pupils' subject progress and achievement is somewhat limited and vague. A tighter and clearer process is needed for this aspect of their responsibility to be properly carried out. It is also important for the heads of year to have regular, scheduled meetings with their year teams, as recommended in the staff handbook, with agenda and action minutes. In turn the heads of year themselves need the opportunity to meet together formally to clarify overall school pastoral objectives and policies. This could give a sharper focus to the obvious fund of caring commitment evident throughout the school. . . .
>
> All form groups have three fifteen-minute registration/ tutorial periods a week, together with fifty minutes each Friday morning, although it appears this period can be

rather too often superseded by other events. In the main, the short tutor periods appear to be used for registration, absence notes, announcements and general quiet socializing. On Mondays lunch money is collected for the week, the form teacher discreetly ticking the names of those entitled to free lunch without calling them out. The longer Friday session is used by some form teachers in some years for aspects of active tutorial work, with an emphasis on life and study skills. However, there is no clear whole-school policy on the use of tutor time in a positive way, although the senior teacher, amongst other tasks, appears to have responsibility for leading the heads of year in the development of a pastoral programme. This task can only be carried out when time for meetings becomes available. Individual initiatives are to be applauded but greater coherence and rigour with the positive engagement of all concerned could have an enhancing and marked impact.

(ILEA, 1986, pp. 10–12)

Not many Tutors will find themselves in schools with such pastoral management as that! However, many of us find difficulty creating the 'greater coherence and rigour' which pastoral management requires.

Training

Our profession makes much of the strength of being a 'qualified teacher', perhaps under-playing the facts that:

- before 1974 a degree in any subject offered qualified teacher status;
- in Maths and Science that continued;
- the PGCE is a very short course, with a very short profes-

sional component, and usually little or nothing on pastoral care.

Indeed it is clear from talking to PGCE and B. Ed. students that very many of them have had little or no preparation for their pastoral responsibilities. Major confirmation of this lack was spelt out in detail by the nationwide study of new teachers in schools by HMI in 1982 which showed that this aspect of initial training tailed dismally behind most others investigated. For instance, whereas only some 21 per cent felt less than well prepared for classroom management, the highest figure, 54 per cent, felt themselves 'not well prepared to undertake pastoral duties' (HMI, 1982). A little later the National Association for Pastoral Care in Education surveyed a large sample of teachers working in schools, and found that as many as 87 per cent 'argued that their initial training contained either a negligible amount of work on pastoral care or nothing at all' (Maher and Best, 1984). And more recently still the National Association summed up the situation:

> Taken as a whole, the evidence suggests that there are few other aspects of the work of secondary schools or of other educational institutions for which so little training is available.
>
> (NAPCE, 1986, p. 14)

More recently, the figures on how well prepared newly trained teachers are for pastoral care show only a small improvement. Secondary probationers were asked in 1987 whether they were 'well prepared to undertake pastoral duties': 36 per cent felt 'well' or 'reasonably well satisfied', 28 per cent 'moderately', and 35 per cent 'less than satisfied' or 'dissatisfied' (HMI, 1988, p. 34).

A very large study of initial training by HMI from 1983 to 1985 showed little preparation for any aspect of pastoral work. The only specific reference to the pastoral role is carefully limited:

> With varying degrees of success, the institutions sought to ensure that the students were well equipped and confident in their knowledge of their specialist subject, practised in various methods of teaching it, and able to fulfil the important pastoral role of looking after the overall welfare of the pupils entrusted to their care.
>
> (HMI, 1987, p. 104)

And the only description of the content of courses over-emphasises one aspect:

> In helping students towards an understanding of their pastoral role, institutions recognised that its foundation must rest on the development of good relations with pupils.
>
> (Ibid.)

This is a truism that covers only a fraction of the content needed in a pastoral care course. It will be seen that even this recognition does not encourage confidence in what is done about helping student teachers. The coverage of personal and social development was politely but cuttingly criticised:

> An important element in the training process is the extent to which individual courses point up the contribution which the subjects of the curriculum can make to the personal and social development of pupils. Evidence of attention to this aspect of the work at secondary level was patchy, and although syllabuses and schemes of work sometimes referred to social and personal development needs,

these were not often explicitly mentioned in the actual presentation of lectures and seminars. In only a small proportion of subject method courses were students being given a clear understanding of their role in relation to personal and social development, and in two-thirds of cases this aspect was not actually being covered. Occasionally, a correlation between subject method and education studies offered good opportunities for some discussion of personal and social development.

(Op. cit., p. 120)

Put together, the 1981 and 1987 figures show that for years a huge proportion of teachers have perceived themselves as having inadequate preparation for pastoral care. *Essentially we have a profession untrained for its central daily tutorial task.*

To make matters worse, very few middle-management responsibility-holders have had any form of initial or in-service work, despite a few good national courses, NAPCE regional meetings, and the annual NAPCE conference. Those who lead the leaders are in an even more perilous plight, according to a training survey (by ILEA Research and Statistics):

Specific courses taken by percentage of senior management:

Topics of courses:	Heads	Deputies	Senior teachers
Management topics	27	21	10
Curriculum planning	19	12	8
Timetabling	3	20	10
Pastoral care and counselling	3	8	3

(Jayne, 1982, pp. 6–7)

It is easier to face the task if we accept the huge gaps in preparation that we all have.

Conclusion

Very many teachers find the tutorial aspect of their professional work very rewarding indeed, and are patently successful despite the difficulties. Very many tutees speak warmly and gratefully of the support, encouragement, and demands of their Tutors. However, I should estimate that, weak teachers apart, the proportion of competent teachers succeeding well as Tutors is lower than that of those succeeding well in their subjects. For instance, an LEA inspection report of a well-regarded and soundly staffed boys' school includes this comment on the tutoring:

> Since most members of staff are tutors, most teach one period of PSE each week. The high degree of commitment of this body of teachers was quite obvious, but sadly some were unsure of teaching processes with which they were unfamiliar and inexperienced. The result was that some lessons offered little of educational value, while in others, a most valid contribution to the personal and social education of pupils was observed and relevant teaching processes were employed.
>
> (ILEA, 1985, p. 15)

Here the problem appears to emanate from the 'PSE' (a 'Tutorial Programme'), and all observation and anecdote confirms the uncomfortably high proportion of Tutors not at ease with this major aspect of their work.

Often, as I outlined earlier, the difficulty derives from the lack of planning, materials, and leadership. Also, though, it derives from the teachers' lack of clarity and strength of vision about tutoring. In some ways, the obvious approach is the simplest and most effective: compare a full-group tutorial session with a subject and use the same techniques:

- What is the intended learning outcome in terms of understanding, attitudes, facts, skills?
- What topic could focus that?
- What learning activities could embody it?
- What learning materials would assist?
- What would be the best shape of the session?

In other words, if you are worried, just think about the aim of the next run of tutor sessions in the way that you would in your own subject specialism, and think up ways of getting the pupils working toward the agreed aim by whatever methods you are most happy with. Don't feel too tied by the specific learning material.

'Group' sometimes confuses. I have used the word to contrast with the one-to-one counselling by Tutors. It indicates that the Tutor is working with the entire Tutor Group, but as in any other part of our timetabled work it does not imply 'whole-class teaching' the whole time. Tutors will sometimes want to talk to the whole Tutor Group, but often pupils will be working in small groups and at other times individually.

The group Tutor's range of skills is different in balance and use from that of many subject specialisms, but there is nothing to be done that ingenious teachers don't already do in their own subjects from time to time at the very least.

The Tutor is nearest to, most often with, and has the widest knowledge of his tutees and should have the closest relationship with them. (Of course, there will be tutees who 'get on better' with other colleagues, but the Tutor–tutee relationship should be the most reliable.) This knowing of tutees and having a close relationship with them is necessary but not sufficient. Be wary of those who say the Tutor's task is 'getting to know his pupils'. That is a means and not an end.

The Tutor is the heart of the school, the specialist whose specialism is bringing everything together, whose subject is the pupil herself, who struggles for the tutee's entitlement, and who enables the pupil to make best use of the school and develop her person. The Tutor will be successful to the extent that he keeps this central vision in mind and builds out of it an over-arching pattern to which all the details relate.

2 Personal and social growth

Introduction

The best definition of pastoral care, that peculiar British educational phrase, is 'personal, educational, and vocational guidance'. (Though the Scottish 'guidance teacher' has a sharper edge.) In a way, the second two parts serve the first:

- 'Educational' guidance is the art of helping the 'child' become a 'student' and thus make best use of school and other (sometimes informal) educational resources. (Chapter 5 explores this in more detail.)
- 'Vocational' guidance needs to start early in schooling and grows naturally out of, and feeds back into, the ideas of 'personal' development.

Thus pastoral care essentially focuses on personal development. In this work of 'personal guidance' and enabling the young person to face that question 'Who am I?', what do we mean by 'personal development'? Is it just a warmly meant but vague notion that pupils will develop on a variety of fronts and that, as each will develop differently, this varied development is indeed 'personal' – particular to that person?

If that were to be so, the claim that the Tutor is the heart of the school would be a weak one as the Tutor would be no more than a facilitator. The phrase means rather: *the further and enhanced development of the tutee as a person.* That is, the Tutor's concern with 'personal' development is so called because it is the very quality of 'person' that the Tutor seeks to help the tutee develop.

One key process in that development is to help tutees achieve 'rational autonomy'. This clearly reduces the teachers' reliance on exhortation and admonition to affect behaviour, because they largely produce only short-term changes in behaviour and ones created for extrinsic reasons. The aim of 'rational autonomy' includes knowledge of self, knowledge of others, and knowledge of outcomes. It is also going to emphasise decision-making. Group tutorial work seeks to facilitate that route to rational autonomy.

That is why I started with my definition: 'A Tutor is a teacher whose subject is the pupil herself.' The task of the Tutor is to enable the pupil gradually but consistently, and through that learning of self, to learn better how to understand others, relate to them, to make good use of the school, and gradually to prepare to take a full place in wider society. The Tutor empowers the tutee.

The idea of a person

What, though, do we mean by the qualities of a person, and is a Tutor going to have time to lift himself above the business of the administrative chores to consider them, still less teach them? Can a Tutor have an overview of the aspects of the personal?

We have all become aware of the pejorative meaning of the phrase 'the hidden curriculum', but we are less clear about why we disapprove and what is the alternative. The objection is that no part of the curriculum should be 'hidden', for if it is indeed not stated openly it is not 'amenable to critical scrutiny or capable of effective translation into practice' (the phrase is Lawrence Stenhouse's, 1975, p. 4). Only if openly defined can the curriculum be debated and agreed (for instance, by parents and governors) and only then consciously built into programmes. As Richard Pring criticises:

> Often, of course, such qualities, traits and knowledge remain only implicit in the exhortations, the daily routine and the relationships of most schools. But they are still there, and curriculum development in this area must at least begin with an attempt to make them explicit and to subject them to analysis and criticism.
>
> (Pring, 1984, p. 25)

In much schooling the qualities being aimed at are taken for granted and even the most major ones are left to the tutee's own guess. A few get declaimed from the assembly platform, but few schools have developed a systematic description of such aims.

In planning the growth of tutees up the years of a tutorial programme, it is necessary to have some analytical framework for our concept of 'the personal'. What aspects of 'a person' are we concerned with?

One sevenfold set of distinctions that draws upon common-sense terminology is by Richard Pring in his valuable book *Personal and Social Education in the Curriculum*:

1 Intellectual virtues
(Those skills and abilities of the mind that allow accurate observation, clear thought, hypothesis, logical argument, and exposition.)

2 Moral virtues
('Dispositions such as modesty, kindness, patience, generosity, which govern the emotions.')

3 Character traits
('Those qualities of the "will" such as perseverance or courage which are separate from (2) and can be a bad thing if linked with a lack of intellectual or moral virtues.')

4 Social competencies
(That is, the skills such as oral, bodily, dressing, understanding situations, handling organisations, which are required to make the first three operational: a person can be intellectually vigorous, morally fine, and generously disposed but sadly incompetent to make anything of the qualities.)

5 Practical knowledge
(Which is necessary also for (4) to operate.)

6 Theoretical knowledge
(The 'concepts, beliefs, principles, insights afforded through theoretical study'.)

7 Personal values
(These are not synonymous with (2) and (3): 'Two people could be equally gentle and considerate but disagree on the value of pacifism.')

(Pring, 1984, pp. 22–4)

Such a model of what makes each of us 'a person' must underlie a programme of tutorial work. The curriculum should look to all seven, and the tutorial team has to find the ways of helping each individual assess his or her own sense of each.

What makes a tutee a developing person is the interaction of each of the seven aspects. The school as a whole will seek to develop all of them, but the Tutor will help make the pupil conscious of them and better able to assess and develop them in the social context.

Thus 'personal development' is not just 'developing personally' but 'developing the person' – and that is the core of pastoral care, which every aspect of the work òf the Tutor must serve.

Reciprocity

However, 'social' development is an inherent part of 'personal' development, and this not only to protect the rights of others, but because my view of myself is deeply affected both by my view of others and by my perception of their view of me. I cannot understand myself without understanding others. A pupil's view of his ethnicity or gender, for instance, substantially results from his view of others and thus mutuality is a strong thread of tutorial work.

The tutorial task thus involves both the skills of relating to others and also the analysis of one's attitude to other people and its relationship with attitude to self. This reciprocity is important.

It is worth remembering that human beings do not always recognise others as 'persons'. Slaves, black people, women, for instance, have been put aside at various times in different societies as lacking the full range of attributes. Such extreme examples will not blind us to the ease with which we write off certain people and occupations as similarly lacking: our tutees share with us the human tendency to refuse to admit the humanity of some others.

For instance, it is an over-simplification to consider prejudice, especially in terms of racism, as if the issue were only one of a person's view of *others*. Few aspects of tutoring reveal the reciprocity of personal development so clearly: view of self and view of others are deeply related.

Peter Newsam, when he was Chairman of the Commission for Racial Equality, put the paradox very clearly. He described racial prejudice as being less the result of our view of the inferiority of others than our view of *ourselves*:

> Racial discrimination does not proceed, on this theory, from any sense of the inferiority of others. It begins from a particular picture of oneself and the group of which one is part. Other groups, other races, may be held to be as intrinsically to be valued as ourselves. That is not the problem with their presence. The prejudice against them derives from their inability to become us and the necessity, on this theory, for us to remain as we are or, in some way, perish.
>
> This is a difficult theory to deal with. Prejudice built on hatred of others is obviously and easily deplorable. Prejudice built on a particular picture, with some attractive features, of oneself is far harder to dislodge.
>
> To sum up: on this analysis, racial prejudice is caused only at second hand by a view of other people. It starts – as it did in grotesque form with Hitler – with an exaggerated and inflexible opinion of oneself. So the world is divided into us and not-us; and any threat to us, through too much influence being given to not-us, means that we come to see not-us as the enemy: a presence ultimately hostile to our security.

(Newsam, 1986, pp. 9–10)

If there is truth in this, no school course which asks young people to address only their views of *others* will be sufficient: tutoring must ask them to reciprocate by addressing their view of themselves, and, conversely, their view of themselves will affect and be affected by their view of others.

Thus the Tutors' task of helping their tutees to sense the 'person' in everyone has two purposes – to help them understand *themselves* and to help them relate to others and work successfully with them. This *reciprocity* is central and the group itself can be developed as a laboratory resource for it: reciprocity with others is partly learned via the activities, conventions, and requirements of tutor-group life. The larger aims and the daily details come together with the Tutor's blending.

Knowing and judging

Our profession properly is heavily concerned with cognitive growth and our lessons so shaped. Substantially, of course, that is as it should be, but not completely. The tutorial role must include that but go well beyond it to an emphasis on attitudes, morality, respect, skills, and the judgement required for decision-making. Many studies in aspects of 'health' education have shown that knowledge is necessary but not sufficient. For instance, a large-scale US study of approaches to changing cigarette-smoking behaviour reported:

Adolescents, therefore, need to be equipped with skills that will permit them to express their own desires and beliefs. Since the peer group is essential to the adolescent's lifestyle, it is imperative that adolescents learn how to express themselves, follow their own convictions . . . and yet not alienate themselves from their peer group.

(Del Greco, 1980, p. 81)

21

That, and similar studies, found that 'facts about' were inadequate; a 'life-skills approach' better enabled the student to develop her decision-making confidence.

Writing for the American Health Foundation, Gilbert Botvin summed up, stressing that, while US knowledge-based programmes succeeded in changing students' knowledge and attitudes about cigarette smoking, they had little impact on actual smoking behaviour: 'Apparently, knowledge of the dangers of cigarette smoking in itself is not a deterrent for most students.' (Botvin et al., 1980, p. 140) His New York study of fourth- and sixth-formers concluded that 'any increases in smoking knowledge played only a minor role in reducing the incidence of new smoking'.

Success in enabling young people to change their actions and not just alter their knowledge related to wider approaches to decision-making:

> The problem of cigarette smoking was addressed indirectly within the larger context of basic life skills. Included were sessions on self-image, decision-making, advertising techniques, coping with anxiety, communication skills, social skills, and assertiveness training.
>
> (Botvin et al., 1980, p. 137)

In other words, young people, like the rest of us, need knowledge; but for us to alter our actions and styles and for us to take hold on ourselves, facts and intellectual understanding are necessary but not sufficient. As one researcher finds from his studies: 'At the core of Health Education is informed decision-making' (Balding, 1987, p. 179).

Thus 'personal growth' requires facts but cannot depend on them alone: growth into rational autonomy requires the ability to judge, to enquire, to reject, to be alone without being lonely, and to be able to decide wisely. As Button succinctly

puts it: 'It is not enough to know, much less to be told.'
(Button, 1987, p. 133)

The constraints of others

An emphasis on 'personal growth' can be misunderstood by
some, who think this means unbridled individualism, everything for oneself. The opposite is true: the Tutor has to help
the tutee recognise and respect the rights of others, to grow
the moral consciousness involved, and to find ways of relating to others in a variety of contexts.

We are all used to reprimanding pupils who hurt others,
shout over others, or are verbally rude. We all seek to encourage respect for other pupils and adults. However, the
Tutor's role is to do more than notice any failures and
reprimand. The Tutor in the Tutor Group enables the tutee
to understand the constraints of different facets of society,
from the playground to the classroom, the corridor to the
street. Conventions are analysed, and their rationale and the
limits of their rationality explored. For instance, the conventional rules of keeping to the left or the right on roads can
be explained in ways that are different from those of greeting
a stranger.

It is part of personal growth to internalise the modes of
working with others, and part of the tutorial task to help the
tutee become *consciously* aware of the constraints of society.
As one writer puts it: 'The road to autonomy is paved
through the stages of constraint and co-operation.' (Kutnick,
1987, p. 70)

We speak of personal growth, and in this book I shall continue to stress the enabling power of the Tutor. However, it
is also clear that all our personal choices are constrained by
social pressures. When I emphasise the Tutor's task of

23

helping tutees 'take control of their own lives', I realise that this will be a power limited by the environment. Social pressures will always be there, though part of the tutorial task is partially to free the individual from 'the prison of the peer group' (the phrase is Alex Dickinson's) largely through self awareness, skills training, and the building of personal esteem. I think of the two pressures, self and society, as having the reciprocal relationship of this wedge diagram:

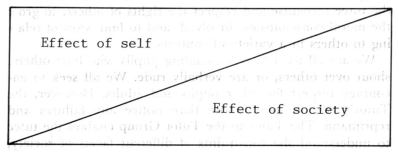

Effect of self

Effect of society

Range of situations

There are few moments when we can truly 'be ourselves' without social pressures reaching us, however tenuously, and there are few moments when the power of the environment is so great that the individual is totally impotent.

Self-assessment

What do young people make of the intermittent and erratic sequence of feedback that is their experience of schooling? And what do we do to help their interpretation? 'The dominant impression of students is that schools are first and foremost places of evaluation, not of learning.' (Covington and Beery, 1976) Sensing this, many schools have tried to de-emphasise testing, and hence are nervous about national assessment. Indeed, many teachers have gone further by attempting to produce motivation and positive inclination by optimistic evaluations that are really unjustified by the performance.

The tutorial task from one point of view is to help tutees make good use of the range of evaluations they receive, and, indeed, even to create additional ones. Young people show variable responses to failure feedback, some deteriorating and others rising to the challenge and even improving their performance in the face of reported failure. The US psychologist, Carol Dweck, has concluded from extensive practical research that 'The variable that consistently predicts response to failure is the child's interpretation of failure – what he thinks caused it and whether he views it as surmountable' (Dweck, 1977, p. 45). She has further shown that encouragement is best achieved not by doses of readily achieved 'success' but by what she calls 'attribution retraining' – that is, helping the pupils see that the negative feedback can be used as a way of analysing what went wrong, and returning to the task with fresh hope. As she puts it:

Children's responses to failure feedback are guided by the manner in which they interpret that feedback. For different children failure has different postdictive and predictive value. Helpless children often view failure as conveying information about their abilities and as signalling continued failure. Persistent, mastery-orientated children view failure as carrying information about specific aspects of their performance that are modifiable.

(Op. cit., p. 48)

The group tutorial work includes as one of its aims enabling the tutee to interpret negative feedback as useful and to arm the tutee with strategies for using criticism. Too often we have attempted this only by exhortation: 'You must all try harder.' The effective Tutor uses group work as well as individual discussion to help the tutee to understand what different reactions (for example, marks, comments) *mean* and how she can make them coherent. Personal growth requires one's understanding of self, but it is not easy to *use* the range of response teachers offer. The Tutor can enable this.

In a sense the fifth-year 'Record of Achievement', now firmly established as national policy, is the summation of the tutorial task up the years to help the tutee's self-understanding, which is in a way a rolling programme of a continuous record of achievement. (For the best overview of Records of Achievement see Hall, 1989.) Thus *LTR* Book 3 (p. 119) has a 'Review' of the Year (see opposite).

The Tutor will establish points for self-evaluative reflection in each year. The Record of Achievement core of negotiated description, self-evaluation, the collection of samples of work, and notes of achievements should not be left to become a desperate final exercise in the fifth year: rather, that is the culmination of such work up the years, indeed starting, as *LTR* Book 1 (p. 56) does, in the first year (see p. 28).

Some of this work will require an explanation of the school's and each department's grading scheme. For instance, for many years the old Inner London Education Authority's primary/secondary transfer scheme 'banded' children as one, two, or three. Very few pupils I found were helped to understand this. Some schools have carefully agreed standardised schemes, and the introduction of national assessment will speed this up and interlock with it. North Westminster uses an effort protocol for effort grades in reporting, as shown on page 29.

Tutors need to give firm, specific tuition on how the school's systems work and what they mean, for example,

LEARN FROM EXPERIENCE

Review the year

In general, whatever the ups and downs have been, by now you will feel more sure of yourself, your decisions for the subjects you have chosen and your attitude towards school.

By the age of fourteen, most students are beginning to show what they are really capable of in school work. You will be better equipped to face and come to terms with:

- how you get on in class;
- the way you approach your work;
- your strengths and particular abilities;
- where you feel you need to put more effort into making improvements.

The learning skills you have tackled over the last two or three years will clearly be producing good results, now.

It is worth looking back on the year. Not just from a personal point of view, but from the point of view of your whole group.

This unit is designed to help you review the year for your Tutor Group as a whole.

ASSIGNMENTS ▷ ▷ ▷ ▷ ▷ ▷ ▷ ▷

1 On your own, draw up a chart with these two headings:
   (a) Problems and difficulties we have faced over the year
   (b) Achievements, improvements and gains we have made over the year.

Then, fill in the chart with different comments under each heading. Remember that you are writing this about your group. It is best not to be personal by mentioning people by name. But, you can mention things that smaller groups within the class have done that have affected the whole class.

2 In groups of four, share the comments you have made in your chart. As far as difficulties and problems are concerned, discuss:
   - why you think they cropped up;
   - how the class dealt with them;
   - whether they were properly dealt with;
   - whether there are any still left to sort out;
   - how they can be avoided in the future.

3 Choose one person to report back one item that you think is worth a special mention.

4 Still in your group of four, discuss achievements and improvements by making a note of:
   - how this helped your Tutor Group;
   - who was encouraging to you;
   - whether any improvements went un-noticed;
   - how your group felt at the time;
   - whether your tutor was told about them.

5 Choose a different person to report back to the class. Decide on one point that you would like to share with the class.

6 Ask your tutor to give her/his view of how your Tutor Group has been this year. Perhaps your tutor could also offer guidance about some of the difficulties you have faced as a group and offer encouragement about your achievements.

7 Finish by each of you saying one thing you would wish for your Tutor Group next year. It could be to do with:
   - the way you get on together;
   - the way others see you as a group;
   - how teachers feel about you;
   - what you would like to do next year;
   - any improvements that could be made;
   - something your tutor could do for you.

Longman Tutorial Resources Book 3, p. 119

HOW AM I DOING?

How am I doing?

You've been at your new school for some time now. And you've learned a lot about how to get on there.

Now is a good time to think back, and to think about how you've been getting on.

Here are some questions and sentences to help you with your thinking. When you've finished them, we'll find a way for you to talk over what you've said with your friends, with your parents, and with your tutor and teachers.

One of the things I've done well at recently has been ....

....

One of the things I've found difficult recently has been ......

....

One of the things I've enjoyed most recently has been ....

The things I'm doing best in are ....

....

and the reason is ....

Things I'm not doing so well in are ....

....

and the reason is...............................

My parents, and/or the adults I live with seemed proud when...............................

I was proud when I ....

EFFORT GRADES

(a) Grades for effort are not, in themselves, grades for behaviour or
attitude. They are to be arrived at by the individual teacher, and are
best thought of as criterion-referenced, for there is no reason why
some years or some classes shouldn't have a higher or lower proportion
of each grade than others. The list below sets out the behaviour
associated with each grade; thus the grades could be thought of as
behaviour measured against our expectation and hopes of pupils'
behaviour. There will be no fixed percentages associated with each
grade.

(b) The following 'behaviour protocol' should be used by class teachers as
a guide to the grades:

A Uses initiative to do work beyond that set; is persistent in the
face of difficulty, tenacious with problems, and energetic in
producing work.

B Completes all the work set, pretty well always on time except when
held back by genuine difficulties; efforts rarely flag.

C Meets all a teacher's basic expectations satisfactorily; tries to
complete and hand in work, and usually manages to; at least follows
classwork lessons; always attempts homework; but has a few off days.

D Offers less work than is required; that completed is frequently
skimpy; doesn't take much responsibility for personal organisation
of work materials; often switches off.

E Doesn't attempt much of the work; also positively refuses some
of it.

It will be seen that 'C' is meeting satisfactorily our basic expectations;
'E' is positively making great efforts to do nothing or near to nothing.

(c) Although individual teachers will establish these grades, HoDs will be
expected to monitor them to ensure that they are not applied
idiosyncratically or punitively, and that they tally with the verbal
descriptions.

An example of an effort protocol

what is the referencing – internal or external, norm or criterion?

As the tutee moves up the years, the review sessions mentioned earlier should become longer, more detailed, and in a sense more 'formal'. It is very important that Record of Achievement reviewing is not left as a sudden change of style and purpose towards the conclusion. One study of reviewing in a school found:

> Evidence from Brant suggests that initially students viewed formal discussions with some apprehension. The following factors can be identified to account for this:
> - the review was unfortunately called 'an interview';
> - it was a unique experience for the student in that, for the majority, it was the first time they had conversed at length with an adult outside their family circle;
> - it was difficult for them to conceive the interaction as a mutually helpful experience when the tutor was seen as an authority figure, that is, he/she shared the discipline function with the head of year and was responsible for writing a character reference;
> - some students were unhappy about their present relationship with a particular tutor on a one-to-one basis.
>
> (Hall, 1989, pp. 61–7)

The second and third points are especially important: the older student should have been helped to *learn* about self-assessment and should in a gradual series of steps have come to 'own' the review session, understand its purpose, and feel comfortable.

'Self-conscious' is a pejorative word in current use, implying 'awkward', 'embarrassed', 'lacking genuineness'. Yet not to be 'conscious of self' should be the unhappy situation. The work of the tutorial programme aims to enable the tutee to be valuably more self-conscious in a positive way. Self-assessment can be 'taught' as part of this, and this involves, as does so much of tutoring, making good use of what the school has to offer.

Morality

Despite the oft-reiterated demands by the public and politicians for schools to 'reinforce morals', there has been rather little exploration of moral education in this country. (Important exceptions are Ungoed-Thomas, 1978; Wilson, 1972; Pring, 1984, Chapter 4; and Weinreich-Haste, 1983.) Indeed, many casual and even a few formally qualified commentators confuse 'moral' education with 'religious' education. The whole school is clearly concerned with moral education in every aspect of the curriculum, the procedures, the regulations, the relationships, and the ethos. However, it is the Tutor who articulates and synthesises this and, above all, brings otherwise random admonition and precept into a deliberately theoretical and disinterested but empathetic consideration.

The idea, developed especially in the USA, of 'values clarification' is a useful one. At its worst, this could be criticised for allowing any outcome provided that the pupil 'knows what he is doing'. On the other hand, the key point is that the Tutor helps pupils clarify their values and rationally make up their own minds.

Many group exercises will informally be following a pattern similar to that of the US moral educator Kohlberg (cf. Kohlberg, 1982), in which a dilemma is put to the Tutor Group and the morality of possible decisions discussed. The material used should include real and fictional examples, from a variety of sources. Education in morality is not, though, primarily education in *what* you should do but *how* you should arrive at your decision.

Thus, frequently in a tutorial programme, actions will be discussed: 'How would you react if . . . ?' 'What do people do when . . . ?' And 'What did she do in that situation?' The Tutor will always have difficulty in focusing not so much on the behaviour as on the cause. Yes, there are universals, though even these can be overruled by higher principles, but these need to be arrived at by focusing on principles, not details. Rules are handy guides but not themselves deeply educative. The Tutor is always (perhaps lightly and certainly tactfully) leading back to the ideas that illuminate rules.

Is it, as some would suggest, arrogant and anyway impossible to be a teacher of virtue? After all, a teacher of the violin can demonstrate his skill on the violin. Is a teacher of virtue expected likewise to demonstrate his personal virtue, and, if he cannot, is he disqualified?

Of course, the answer is that a Tutor is not qualified to lead personal education primarily by her own demonstrable success in leading a successful life but, rather, in her ability to lead young people to face problems, see what is the moral issue, focus questions, gather data, and move towards a rational decision.

In this process of enabling personal growth, the Tutor is using the group as a whole, stimulated by issues, data, texts, and ideas put before it, to help each of its members grow in her person.

Particular events, episodes in the life of the Tutor Group, and individual anecdotes and enquiries will be sympathetically but disinterestedly discussed. However, the Tutor will help the tutees to weave the threads of the range of their lives and their chance experiences into the warp and weft of a fabric that is for each her own and has a coherent strength.

The process of tutoring is empowering the tutee, but with the giving of self-power must go the development of the ability to be sensitive and appropriately generous. Morality in its widest sense is at the heart of tutoring.

Conclusion

By placing the growth of the child as a student and as a person at the centre of tutoring, the school is fulfilling one of its major aims. Through that concept of personal growth, and its social imperative, the Tutor can find the criteria against which her priorities can be judged and by which the details of every action can be shaped. It is from this centre that the heart of group activity in tutorial work grows.

One of the pioneers of group tutorial work in this country, Leslie Button, defined it thus:

> Developmental group work is a way of helping people in their personal growth and development, in their social skills and in the kind of relationships they establish with other people. Its purpose is to provide individuals with opportunities to relate to others in supportive groups, to try out new social approaches and to experiment in new roles. Care, concern and the development of responsible attitudes are basic to the work.
>
> (Button, 1987, p. 130)

If the Tutor is a teacher whose subject is the pupil herself, the aim of that 'subject' is the growth of the tutee as a person in society, and all the ways and actions of the Tutor must be congruent with that aim: everything the Tutor initiates and is required to do must be shaped to work towards the social and personal growth of her tutees.

3 Managing the Tutor Group

'It's funny how teachers make out the tutorial period's important, but they don't do anything in it!'

(Secondary-school pupil)

Introduction

With what can look like an insubstantial and vague task, but one weighed down by a plethora of minor 'business', and with their minds on the challenge of the day's subject teaching, Tutors often do not know what to do with their group other than 'call' the register, chase missing absence notes, and issue reprimands and the occasional praise for helpfulness. The pupil quoted above speaks for many: what is supposed to be going on?

There is, firstly, a tension between individual casework and group work and, secondly, between the proactive and the reactive. The struggle is to respond sensitively to individual needs: 'Please, Miss, my maths teacher said . . .', whilst not being dominated by reacting to the reported worries of your tutees or the complaints about them from your colleagues.

As a subject teacher your aims are fairly homogeneous, and even convergent: you know where you are going. However strongly interested you are in each of the pupils as individuals, the prime intention is clearly that the pupil should achieve the curriculum goals of the subject. The subject curriculum gives a strong direction, a series of steps, an established pedagogy, and learning material. Thus the management of the class derives from a generally well-understood aim, sequence, and method. Conversely, the Tutor's 'subject' lies substantially inside each tutee and thus the course of the tutor-group work is likely to be buffeted by what happens to those individuals. The art of managing a Tutor Group is to balance sensitivity to their daily demands with an over-arching sense of direction derived from the basic purpose of personal and social growth.

Working together

We label twenty-five or thirty pupils as a 'Tutor Group' but of course being designated to go to the same room does not make those pupils automatically into a working group. One characteristic of a successful Tutor Group is that it is self-evaluative as well as self-supportive.

The Tutor can make the tutor room an analogy for the social relationship being developed. The tutor room is, as it were, the 'laboratory' of pastoral care, and the tutees both the scientists and the experimental material. The tutees learn about personal and social development by a variety of modes, of which a key one is the working of their group and the individual place each has within it. In this way, the reception and support of a new pupil is carried out not only to help that pupil but also as a paradigm of the helping of people everywhere. At the same time the full reception of that new pupil involves all the pupils examining themselves, the group, and the school: you cannot explain to a newcomer that which you do not understand. Thus everyone gains from the proper reception of a newcomer.

Similarly, if a member of the group is, say, having continuous difficulty with lateness, the group, or members of it, can be asked to discuss this, and the latecomer helped to help herself by group advice and support.

In these and a myriad of other examples the tutees are learning 'personal and social development' through working with each other. This will rarely happen by chance, and in many groups the opposite is the style of the group: groups can be self-destructive. The Tutor can facilitate the supportive working together by a combination of approaches:

- The inclusion of the general subject of working as a group in discussion and group activities. For instance, separately from any specific issue, the principles can be explored: to what extent can a group help an individual?
- The planning of a group approach to a particular event, such as the leaving of one of the group, a religious festival, or a family event.
- Looking back on an event and analysing how well the group worked together.

Group projects can also focus on:

- group activities (for example, the end-of-year party);
- other teachers (for example, how to negotiate a changed homework pattern, or how to handle the situation of a teacher who can't control the class);
- the tutor room (for example, displays);
- events in the lives of members (for example, birthdays or births of sisters or brothers).

The Tutor should seek constantly to help the members of the group develop as a group.

Administration

'Administration' is normally a pejorative word. Tutors describe many of the tasks assigned to them as 'mere administration' and show their dislike by hurrying through them and treating them as depressing chores: issuing letters, checking homework diaries, checking addresses, arranging for medicals, . . . and so on. The tutees rapidly pick up this attitude, the chores take over the programme, tutoring becomes a bore, and, most important, opportunities are missed.

One trouble is that this administration appears to come down from 'the hierarchy', 'them', or 'the school', and not relate to the tutees' needs. Indeed, often these tasks appear even worse: they positively come between the Tutor and tutee, not merely chores but blocks.

This could be the fault of the administration of the school, giving unnecessary clerical tasks to Tutors (for example, sorting report slips into pupils' packs) or giving only the boring procedural end of a task without its more rewarding professional end (for example, checking family addresses and sending circulars, but not having responsibility for relationship with the home). Sometimes, sadly, it appears pastoral team leaders simply do not brief their Tutors well or take them sufficiently into their confidence.

However, the difficulties can be avoided. What look like 'mere' administrative tasks should be made educationally significant by being woven into the programme – thus checking home addresses and telephone numbers is not a 'chore' but part of learning about communal and institutional support and responsibility. Similarly the use of the final brief tutorial of the day for checking the setting and preparation for the evening's homework is part of the study-skills aspect of group tutoring.

Whilst the expeditious announcement of, say, BCG tests should not be a cue for a lecture on preventative medicine, each of the necessary tasks can be adroitly set in the context of 'why?', and related to the over-arching tutorial aims of personal and social growth.

For instance, the Tutors of one part of a school were required to arrange for their groups to elect a representative for the 'School Council', a pupil consultative organisation. A Tutor could simply announce it as an afterthought, perfunctorily ask for suggestions, and then a vote by show of hands – 'Business over', thank heavens!

Contrasted with that 'chores' approach, I observed a two-session approach with a first-year group, in the first of which the Tutor reminded the group that in many walks of life, such as clubs and organisations, but especially in our government, 'representatives' are elected. 'Represent' – to 'present' or give, 're-' – again. If this group were to be 'represented' by one member to speak for all at meetings, what *qualities* should that person have?

To help the tutees consider what they wanted from *their* representative, the Tutor devised a worksheet (opposite) with a choice of approaches a representative might have. Some could be easily dismissed as silly. Others, like consulting the head of Fabric over the issue of school ties had a seductive but a spurious attraction. There were then a pair that needed careful thought. The tutees discussed their choice in small groups, and at the end the Tutor pooled their arguments. Only in the *next* tutorial session did the nominating and voting start. Thus the Tutor seized a school 'administrative requirement' and made it into a group exercise in personal and social education.

A final example is the daily routine of 'calling the register'. Undoubtedly the regular register-checking is very important, both for the care of the tutee and the legal requirement on

ELECTIONS TO THE SCHOOL COUNCIL

This week you will be voting for two students from IP3 to be Student
Representatives on the School Council. The Representatives – one girl
and one boy – will speak on behalf of the whole tutor group, making
suggestions about how to improve the school and solve problems.

Here are some qualities that the Class Representative might have.

How do you rate these qualities?

	Very Important	Important	Not Important
Are they:			
a Strong and physically fit			
b Good with words			
c Respected by the class			
d Good at listening to other people's opinions			
e Good at explaining her/his opinion			
f Good-looking			
g Smartly dressed			
h Punctual			

Supposing the school made a new rule that next term all girls would have
to wear a school tie, as they do in some other schools.
Here are some things that a Student Representative might do. What does
your group think of these ideas?

a Tell everyone in the class what she/he thought.
b Ask all the girls what they thought about the new rule, and report to
  the next School Council meeting.
c Ask girls and boys what they thought about the new rule, and report to
  the School Council.
d Not speak to anyone about the new rule.
e Give his/her opinion to the Head of Fabric.
f Give his/her opinion at the School Council, without asking what anyone
  else thought.

the school. So enshrined is this in professional mythology that 'taking a register' is the jargon phrase in some schools synonymous with 'lead a tutorial session', as if the register check were the main activity. In many Tutor Groups the tutees are seated silently with no activity and no announcement of a topic or introduction to think about: then, as solemnly and sometimes as slowly as possible, each name is ritually called and answered.

In others, though, whilst the same message of the importance of the accurate check by a designated time is conveyed, the tutees are welcomed first by a reminder about the purpose of that session: 'Today we are continuing our work on how to make complaints effectively.' A task or material to consider awaits them on the board, on the overhead projector, or on a hand-out. After an introduction to this stage of the topic and the setting of a simple thought-provoking task, the Tutor says: 'While you're working out which of those you think would offend least, I'll be checking the register and collecting notes from the two of you absent yesterday.' Thus the register administration is deftly knitted into the tutorial session – as it would be into a good subject lesson.

The effective Tutor, then, either subordinates the administration to the tutorial task or, better still, *uses* it as part of the heart of tutoring.

Tutorial activities

Many of the units in tutorial programmes are planned to stimulate activity by the tutees. There is, of course, no virtue in activity for activity's sake: perhaps in search of peace we too often mistake mere doing for learning. It is especially important in tutorial work that the tutee's *understanding* is engaged at as deep a level as possible. The Tutor needs to select activities that will stimulate a consideration and reconsideration by the tutee of her attitudes and perceptions.

For instance, *LTR* Book 1 naturally starts, as many Tutors would, with developing an understanding of the new pupil's school and how a pupil can begin to make best use of it. The approach is not overtly explanatory but takes the tutee via an active reflection on previous visits to the school, comparisons of expectation, how it's turning out, and the working out of how to help each other. The unit, therefore, has a range of simple and easy-to-handle things for the tutees to do: questions, small investigations, and plans. The material in the book is designed to help the tutees understand their experience and grow from it. Quick advice and short-circuited ways round the almost inevitable difficulties of a new school should be complemented by the inner reflection that changes attitudes – and which makes *this* experience more than just getting settled into a school: it is, as so much group tutorial work, a paradigm for life.

Similarly, the unit on homework in *LTR* Book 1 (p. 32) leads the tutee to scrutinise his work, to question, to study the ways of others in the group, and to answer questions about two case studies. The activity of questioning others is designed to deepen the understanding of self.

Very few of the activities suggested in the units of any tutorial programme will be found difficult to handle in the tutor room; indeed most of them are within the normal repertoire of subject teachers. However, many Tutors may not have experience of deploying the full range of the repertoire of teaching techniques or of moving from one technique to another so flexibly as is required for tutoring. The activities are presented so that the Tutor Group has a contrasting range: reading, individual writing, small-group discussion, paired discussion, investigation. Tutors will normally find it best to exploit this variety so as to vary the *texture* of the tutorial sessions: it is easy to slip into a repetitive routine in which every session feels the same to your tutees – read, talk, write, for instance, in an invariable sequence.

The opposite page has an extract from *LTR* Book 2 (p. 27). The first section could be read by pupils or introduced by the Tutor. Assignment 1 gives four situations and suggests each tutee should write an estimate of her likely response. The emphasis given by the Tutor has to be on the *honesty* of the tutee's speculation, not on the 'correctness' of the response. The key activity is 'get a friend to check what you've written and see if you've been accurate and honest'. *This* is what needs most time and will both depend on the tutor group atmosphere and trust and, very importantly, contribute to it by increasing self- and mutual understanding.

Activities must not be merely text- and worksheet-based. Indeed, relating to people is self-evidently a necessary way of developing *social* education. Sometimes tutees should be relating to each other in simple simulations: 'You are . . . and have to greet . . . .' Whenever possible, though, there should be interaction with people outside the group: other students, staff of the school, and visitors. Greeting, briefing, interviewing, and introducing are important learning experiences that embody aspects of the curriculum content of pastoral care.

As often as possible the activities should be real: boredom by a thousand simulations is all too easy. For instance, there will be members in hospital, families ready for celebrations, members of staff needing help, members of the community offering help. Phone-calls, letters, visits, and visitors need planning, carrying out, and reflecting on.

The skilled Tutor will deploy a varied repertoire of activities that develop the personal growth of the tutees.

NOW YOU'RE A SECOND YEAR

ASSIGNMENTS ▷ ▷ ▷ ▷ ▷ ▷ ▷ ▷ ▷ ▷ ▷ ▷ ▷

1 Now see what you think is the most likely response you would make to the following situations. When you've finished, get a friend to check what you've written and see if you've been accurate and honest. You can do the same for her or him.

- Everyone in the class is told off and given a detention for misbehaviour, but you know you were working perfectly well.
- You're told off quite rightly for not completing your homework but you don't like the teacher anyway and you feel fed-up.
- You're frantically finishing off a piece of work you've enjoyed when it's you who's asked to collect up everyone's books before the end of the lesson.
- You've been getting into trouble for not having a pen with you, but this time it really isn't your fault – you have a good excuse – but nobody's interested!

2 Think of a lesson when you were getting on well with the teacher and feeling pleased with how things were going. With a friend, see if you can remember the following details:

- What was the lesson about?
- How did the teacher explain it?
- What were you expected to do or to contribute?
- Were you fully up to date with all your work when the lesson started?
- Were you sitting with a group or with a particular person likely to help you concentrate?
- Did you get any praise and encouragement from the teacher?
- Was there anything you thought or said or did which especially made you feel good?
- Were there any classroom rules for this subject, with this teacher, that helped you work well?
- Can you use any of the elements of this good lesson to help out in other lessons? Think of a lesson in which things didn't go so well: what made the difference? How could you have helped to make it any better?

Longman Tutorial Resources Book 2, p. 27

Paired and small-group work

Most, but not all, subject teachers use small-group work for discussion and planning. However, each subject tends to have its own convention and purpose for this. Teachers of Craft, Design and Technology, for instance, are used to groups of, perhaps, two or three, planning design solutions to specific briefs. Often such discussion work is at its best in this subject, perhaps because of the clarity of the end-product required: an agreed design or evaluation. Such teachers will bring especial skills to the tutorial but may find the purpose of some of the tutorial discussion tasks harder to handle as they may appear more intangible.

There is the fundamental question of why put the tutees into groups? What are we aiming at? What is intended? Are the tutees merely expected to work in groups or to do group-work? As one fascinating study puts it:

> The descriptors 'groupwork' and 'work in groups' are often used synonymously – regardless of whether students are intended to work collaboratively or independently and of how their tasks are structured. This is where the potential for confusion begins.
>
> (Ryder and Campbell, 1988, p. 22)

'Groupwork' and 'work in groups', they rightly stress:

> are actually distinct – if related – activities, so that using the terms interchangeably can lead to false and poten-tially damaging claims and criticisms being made of each. This is not merely a semantic quibble. For the health of groupwork, as well as that of work in groups, clarity is paramount. It is not so much that it matters which par-ticular labels people use, as long as practitioners under-

stand what they are doing and what they hope to achieve by doing it.

(Op. cit., p. 23)

'Working in groups' is a mere description of the disposition of pupils. 'Groupwork' is the *use* of the group experience as a resource for the learning of its members. For a task to be carried out together is, of course, acceptable. On the other hand when students are deliberately expected to interact with one another, share a common aim, and jointly reflect on their achievement, something else is happening: the members of the group are learning something from the group itself. In these cases, the group, its members and their interaction are part of the *learning material* as well as the method.

The Tutor planning an assignment will not let the tutees break into groups as a matter of habit, but will use the tutor room as a laboratory of pastoral care, the group as both scientist and material, finding ways of *using* the group to increase personal and inter-personal understanding.

The first question about small-group work is the composition of the groups. Most Tutors let their tutees choose their own seats and thus most neighbours are self-chosen friendship groups. For some discussions this is helpful – the pupils already know each other well. On other occasions, though, this old familiarity acts as an unseen barrier to fresh thinking: the well-established friends have stereo-typical views of each other, have cast each other into permanent roles, and cannot bring fresh responses to the focus of the work. They know each other so well there is no re-knowing possible; they have had so many personal and jokey conversations that they cannot bring a new language to analyse their behaviour.

It is wise, therefore, to establish early in tutorial work that there will be a variety of groupings, and why this is good. Sometimes they will be self-chosen and at other times the

45

Tutor will choose. Sometimes the Tutor will choose at random and at other times deliberately pair those who do not usually work together. Pupils can become unwitting prisoners of their 'best friends' and the exploration of much tutorial activity needs to work outside as well as inside these established friendship patterns. Sometimes they will be mixed-sex groups and sometimes single-sex.

There is a temptation for self-chosen groups to have one or two well-known loquacious pupils and a very quiet one. It *can* be good for reticent pupils to be in with the verbally assured, but it can also inhibit them further. Two normally silent pupils together for an assignment virtually forces each of them to talk. Thus a variety of criteria should be used in composing groups – routine composition can be unwise.

Logically, the mode of grouping should reflect the purpose of the activity. On occasions, arbitrary random groups will work, for instance for devising a solution to a life-skills problem. On other occasions self-chosen groups work better. The key is to ensure that the group has a task, briefing, materials, and a composition that encourage mutual scrutiny and understanding.

Assignments

As in many aspects of education, the key is not the exposition but the assignment. The pupil passes through a battery of assignments but does not always grasp the purpose.

In setting the discussion assignment, Tutors will need to use the precision of a science or humanities teacher in making clear what the *point* is and what *product* the discussion is to lead to. In the apparently intangible world of personal and social development, it is too tempting to let every conversation be about very similar things and for routine remarks

LEARN FROM EXPERIENCE

Micklemus Blackman writes about the first time he went gliding:

When it was my turn to fly I was excited but also quite nervous. The glider was pulled up by a cable and I wasn't sure whether this cable was safe as it had snapped before.

I did some checks with the instructor to make sure the instruments and controls were still working.

The cable was on and we made sure that the glider was all clear above and behind. We took up the slack in the cable. 'All out', he said, which means that the cable car has to pull in the cable fast enough for the glider to take off.

I felt my stomach roll over and my head swirled. Then the glider left the ground and this is when the flight was at its bumpiest.

The instructor pulled a little cable which made the tow cable detach from the glider. We bumped and swerved. For a second I thought we were going to crash. It'll take me some time to go solo.

ASSIGNMENTS ▷ ▷ ▷ ▷ ▷ ▷ ▷ ▷ ▷ ▷ ▷ ▷ ▷

1 What helps you look forward to new experiences?
  In your groups discuss how important you think the following points are:
  - It's important to congratulate yourself when you've done something new, or something that you're proud of.
  - Encouragement from others is more likely to help you see your way forward.
  - Friends around you who are willing to join in and share new activities with you often act as a support.
  - If you trust the people you're with then you're more likely to experiment and still feel safe.

2 Here are some possible new situations that you could find yourself in. Each group can take one example and jot down all the questions which need to be answered beforehand:
  - joining a club   • your first date
  - going abroad   • staying away from home

  Then think about what you would like to happen to make you feel safer and more self assured.

Longman Tutorial Resources Book 3, p. 107

to be rehearsed. Hence the wording of the discussion assignments has to be very carefully sharpened. For instance, in the unit 'Learn from experience' in *LTR* Book 3 (p. 107) the first assignment is not baldly: 'How should you prepare for a new experience?', but a more precise list of options is offered to help the tutees break new ground in their thinking (see p. 47).

Tutors would be well advised to highlight the focus of the task 'Discuss how important you think the following points are', and not use the text as a mere springboard for a general discussion on new experiences.

Guidance can be given from time to time on discussion methods. For instance, one of the hardest intellectual tasks for the secondary student is to move away from a narrative-dominated way of speaking to a more abstract analytic mode in which the anecdote is an illustration, not an end in itself. Children are great, if sometimes interminable, story-tellers. Do not let the tutorial work sink under a string of episodes!

4 From exhortation to enabling

Introduction

Childhood is a journey through admonition, exhortation, and advice. This is intensified at school, and the Tutor can easily become chief exhorter – not only with her own demands but also as a mouthpiece for the massed complaints of the range of subject teachers! Not only is a barrage of exhortation unlikely to change the tutee, except at the margins and for a few, but the tutor session risks becoming little more than a tirade of such exhortation.

Many teachers in their subject capacity almost unconsciously look to those with pastoral responsibilities to control and discipline their pupils by remote control. They nobble you in the coffee queue and send notes suggesting, 'That Tracey of yours is wasting her time in my lessons – and making my teaching difficult – do something about it!' Often they want immediate effects without any inner change, or, equally perversely, wholesale character and personality changes!

This is a major example of how the Tutor can be over-burdened by the immediate 'business' of the task and be tempted to short-circuit the educational core of the tutorial role.

Much of the art of tutoring is foreseeing likely problems and finding active and thought-provoking ways of preparing for them. The exhortation or warning may be necessary ('When you find . . ., don't whatever you do . . . .'), but this approach is not sufficient. Ways of analysing and thus enabling tutees to devise a repertoire of strategies for themselves need to be found.

Of course, this does not apply only to difficulties and things that go wrong. The tutorial programme that implicitly portrays life as a journey of travail, facing 'problems' in which drink, drugs, sex, indiscipline, and worry are the landmarks of growth, is inaccurate and unhelpful – but common! Conversely, the work of a Tutor Group should look forward to and relish the quiet pleasures, happinesses, and excitements of life. Morality is not a torture of admonitions but a growth through the pleasure of illuminated choice; relationships are not a series of difficulties, but a revelation of satisfaction and reciprocity.

Learning about learning

One of the most important aspects of the Tutor's role is helping pupils to see how they can make good use of teachers, support staff, resources, and the organisation of the school. The school organisation is in many ways a microcosm that faithfully reflects the other great societal bureaucracies of, for example, the health service, borough councils, the police, the banks, or large commercial organisations. Teaching pupils how to understand the school organisation and make best use of it is also teaching them how to make best use of those other organisations. Such tutoring is in a complementary way best done both by the group sessions of the tutorial programme and by individual advice and counselling on coping with other staff, routines, and choices.

A central part of this is assisting the tutees to reflect on their lessons, the teachers' aims, the methods used, and the pupil's own learning approach and success. If a tutorial session focusing on this is to be more than a jocular repetition of conventional pupil jibes, a deliberate input is required.

Pupils and teachers lack a shared technical language for talking about pedogogy. The pupil's vernacular ('boring', 'just keep writing') is both insufficiently comprehensive or precise. Teachers' jargon curiously has the same failings: few of us have engaged in classroom analysis of teaching. Much of our vocabulary is also vague: for example, 'discussion work'. Jean Ruddock, Professor of Education at Sheffield University, experimented with preparing pupils for a pedagogical change (to enquiry-based history learning) by a special conference for the pupils. She criticised her own arrangements as not providing a way of analysing and discussing teaching and learning. Subsequently she observed:

> Pupils noticed — but did not discuss with their teacher — occasional shortcomings in the new teaching style: 'When we first started we didn't do any writing — no writing at all. He just talked to us. It was rather boring.' The pupils were not able to go further. What they lacked was a shared language for talking about the new pedagogy — the reflexive language of critique which seems to come from the analysis of oneself and one's peers at work.
>
> (Ruddock, 1983, p. 40)

Pupils need, if they are to be successful *pupils*, 'the readiness and the words to talk publicly about learning' (Op. cit., p. 41). Part of the tutorial programme is to provide this possibility.

The Tutor Group is also the laboratory of the understanding of learning. Pupils bring expectations of what 'lessons' are going to be like, indeed *should* be like. For instance, pupils coming to secondary school for the first time have strong ideas about how 'difficult' work will be – and are often disappointed (cf. the ILEA Secondary Transfer Project, Bulletins 2 and 6). A key tutorial task is to help tutees understand their expectations and to match these against the teachers' plans.

Ideally, the Tutor should work with her subject colleagues preparing for new steps and for change. Jean Ruddock has described the conservatism of pupil groups:

> Pupils, however, are not without power, and their power, which is rooted in long experience of teachers and teaching, can be used to protect themselves against change. If the norms of classroom behaviour are suddenly changed and a new mode of learning introduced, then it is not surprising if pupils seek to reinstate the familiar, the comfortably predictable, and through the power of group pressure lure the teacher back into recognisable routines. Pupils can represent, albeit unwittingly, a conservative force in the classroom.
>
> (Ruddock, 1983, p. 32)

The Tutor, I submit, can harness this 'long experience of teachers and teaching', help make it more conscious, assist the tutees to unpick it and consider component parts, and above all help tutees to control their contribution to the 'group pressure'.

Homework: an example

Homework failure is an obvious example: the Tutor must of course support his colleagues and help the tutees meet their educational targets. However, the Tutor's central task is not merely to get *this* homework settled, or *that* done on time. In this process the Tutor has to keep the educational task of enabling the tutee to understand herself and develop her skills in how to make decisions and take control of time and self.

This is not going to be helped merely by retrospective chiding prompted by subject teachers. The Tutor needs to look ahead, help the tutee to think, and to internalise an understanding of how to handle the challenge of the difficult.

One Tutor of a first-year group, for instance, led a session early in the new term, asking each tutee to review the last few days: how much time had each tutee given to the assignments? Which tutees had not completed a piece of work? What had caused difficulties? The Tutor built up a list of the reasons given on the board, and the group as a whole discussed the justification for each reason, getting the Tutor to erase the rejected reasons.

The Tutor had prepared a multiple-choice work-sheet and in small groups the tutees discussed the pros and cons of each answer. They were considering and devising planning behaviour. You will see on page 54 that there are some obviously discardable answers, but many that need pondering.

Every week cannot see a full session of analysis like this, but, for instance early in the second year, that time of possible lull in enthusiasm, a Tutor would want to ask the tutees in a structured way to reconsider their homework approaches. The first part of such an examination, from *LTR* Book 2 (p. 10), is shown on page 55.

Over the run of a term, of course, the kind of thinking and self-scrutiny explored in such a session would need to be encouraged further. The Tutor would use a few moments at the end of the day to establish the group's assignments; he would have tutees look at each other's work at the start of

Homework

Your teacher has not set any homework. Do you:

(a) keep quiet hoping he has forgotten?
(b) ask for some?
(c) write 'none set'?
(d) do your own for half an hour?

You can't copy down the work in time. Do you:

(a) try to remember it?
(b) tell your tutor?
(c) not do the homework?
(d) ask the teacher to write it up earlier next time?

When do you do it?

(a) Whenever you feel like it.
(b) While watching TV.
(c) The same time each night.
(d) When you are told to.

Where do you do it?

(a) In your room alone.
(b) In the library.
(c) At a friend's house.
(d) In the same room as the TV.

Who helps?

(a) Nobody, you just hand in what you can do.
(b) You get help before you start.
(c) You show it to someone to check after you finish.
(d) You copy the bits you couldn't do from a friend.

NOW YOU'RE A SECOND YEAR

Organise your homework

Write out your homework timetable from memory on a spare piece of paper, then check it.
Did you get it right?

Homework is set every night. Sometimes it must be handed in the next day, and on other occasions it's for the next lesson, which might be two days later or even the next week. This means you need to know not just which night it's set but which day you have to hand it in. What time you can reasonably expect to get started each night is another vital piece of information.
Some people have jobs to do to help at home, like getting vegetables ready for the evening meal or collecting a younger brother or sister.

Some people make a sandwich and turn the television on or go out with friends. In some families, the same things happen each night and a homework routine is easy to get into. Other families have different things happening: one person goes off to a club or starts a night shift, or an auntie comes round. Then, getting into a homework routine is much harder.

▷ Ask yourself these questions:

• Is there any time in the week when I know in advance it will be impossible to do my homework (for example, because I always have to visit my gran on Wednesdays)?
• Is there anything I like to do straight after school (like going swimming)?
• Is there a television programme I like to watch or a club I like to go to each week and I know I'll want to spend time on that?
• What's the latest time I can work to and still have a break before I go to bed?

Now work out a homework timetable which contains this information. It might look something like this:

Work to be given in on:

Monday	Tuesday	Wednesday	Thursday	Friday
Maths Science	English			
3.30–4.30 Swimming 5.00–5.45 English	3.30 Gran always comes round.			

the day; he could arrange for various members of the group to be in charge of certain reminders.

The art, though, is to avoid merely harrying and to enable the tutees to think and plan.

Information-handling and study skills

The Tutor's work enabling the tutee to learn more effectively will often properly engage with the immediate and the actuality of a particular problem of procedure, an individual assignment, an individual teacher, or a detailed skill. The previous account of approaches to homework, though, shows how the Tutor moves from the particular to the general and back again. Without this standing back, comtemplating, analysing, and generalising before re-engagement, the Tutor risks providing the tutees with only a reactive and fragmented series of raids on the coasts of learning – leaving the heartlands unpenetrated and the overall landscape unmapped.

The real tutorial task is deeper and wider – and much more difficult – than exhorting the tutee to 'Work harder!' or encouraging her with snippets of advice as a project stumbles forward for this subject or that. The Tutor will endeavour to enable the tutee to rise above the needs of assignment after assignment and understand, and then take control of, his own learning process. Ideally, the individual subject teacher will be giving clear instruction and practice on the skills required for the tasks when they are required and in the relevant context. Usually such tuition is given solely in context to help the student through the particular learning encounter, rather than helping him find a way to generalise. The rare student will develop her own understanding of what is required and create almost spontaneously

an analysis and synthesis. These students will be the successful ones, the more so as they reach higher levels.

For most students, though, this will not happen unless the
school includes a deliberate understanding of information-
handling skills in the curriculum – that is an intended
learning outcome. The good teacher of History is a teacher
of thinking about issues, assessing evidence, searching out
arguments, and arranging ideas and information in History;
similarly, the good teacher of Science is teaching not only the
answers of Science, but more importantly the method of handling scientific enquiries, the preliminary thinking towards a
hypothesis, the literature search for current knowledge, the
devising of an enquiry, and the weighing of evidence. These
aspects of the curriculum are best thought of as 'information-
handling skills'. They have a remarkable stability across
'subjects', and are more helpfully thought of as 'cross-cur-
riculum skills' (a DES/NCC phrase) than as 'subjects'
themselves.

The phrase 'information-handling skills' was first widely
used in a British Library/Schools Council study (see Marland, *Information Skills in the Secondary Curriculum*, 1981) to
cover the intellectual tasks at the heart of most assignments
from simple homework pieces to lengthy GCSE or A-Level
research studies that involve posing a question, seeking
evidence, and reporting on it. There is a real sense in which
a whole range of adult activities, from, say, writing this book
to preparing an oral presentation to a staff committee, paral-
lels the stream of tasks set throughout the secondary school.
Each can be seen as having in it the same sequence of question steps, even though some assignments speed simply
through some of the steps and enlarge the importance of
others. The nine-fold categorisation of the question steps
from that British Library/Schools Council study is most
usually used as a convenient conceptual working model.

Opposite is the version phrased by Ann Irving in her very useful book *Study and Information Skills Across the Curriculum* (Irving, 1985, pp. 31–2).

Ideally, then, there should be a whole-school policy on the teaching of information-handling skills, with specific tuition and practice in most of the timetabled separate 'subjects'. This is an example of what the DES means when it says of the National Curriculum and its foundation subjects that 'other subjects and cross-curricular themes can and should figure in schemes of work covering the whole curriculum' (DES, 1989, para. 4.3).

Within such an overall plan, the Tutor has a pivotal role in enabling the tutee to develop a central understanding of information-handling and to focus on the range of skills required. The Tutor has the curriculum overview and brings to that the detailed knowledge of the tutee and her modes of working. Consequently, the Tutor is best placed to consolidate and make coherent the disparate learning experiences of the timetable. She can help the tutee stand back, observe the techniques required by the assignments in each subject, see what they have in common and how they differ, and make a coherent inner model of the information-handling process.

The Tutor will probably start by gathering from the tutees a selection of assignments from, say, Science, History, Technology, and English. What is the heart of each assignment? What have they got in common? How does one set about them? Which is the most difficult stage in each? (For instance, sometimes it is finding the sources of facts and ideas, on other occasions understanding the source material when it has been found, on other occasions knowing what to cast aside, and often deciding in which order to re-arrange the facts and ideas.) The Tutor is inviting the tutees to stand back from the *subject*, to put the *content* aside, and, most

Step 1

Formulation and analysis of the information need
What do I need to do?

Step 2

Identification and appraisal of likely sources of information
Where could I go?

Step 3

Tracing and locating individual resources
How do I get to the information?

Step 4

Examining, selecting, and rejecting individual resources
Which resources shall I use?

Step 5

Interrogating, or using, individual resources
How shall I use the resources?

Step 6

Recording and storing information
What shall I make a record of?

Step 7

Interpretation, analysis, synthesis and evaluation of information
Have I got the information I need?

Step 8

Shape, presentation, and communication of information
How should I present it?

Step 9

Evaluation of the assignment
What have I achieved?

The nine question steps in information-handling

importantly, to be free of the tension of completing the work, but instead to reflect on the *process*. The Tutor is thus enabling the tutee to understand the needs of assignments in general and her own skills, and thus to take a grasp of learning.

Without requiring specific school 'subject' knowledge or expertise, the Tutor will sometimes concentrate on one or more of the question steps, and is uniquely placed in the school to compare and contrast these steps in the contexts of different subjects. For instance, the Tutor might spend a session on 'Step 2: Identification and appraisal of likely sources of information' with the prompting question 'Where could I go?' What sources are available when you're trying to find something out? When is it sensible to ask someone? Who is it sensible to ask? When is quoting 'research' and 'scholarly' and when is it 'lazy' or even 'plagiarism'? What are the advantages of journals, newspapers, encyclopedias?

Another session might be on 'Step 6: What shall I make a record of?' What forms of note-making are there? When is photocopying better than note-making? What are the advantages of lined paper against plain; cards against paper; ring-binders against folders? What ways can be used to make the points noted easier to re-organise later? Tutees can compare each other's recording techniques and describe what appear to be the good and bad points. There is no 'right' method, but tutees can be made more conscious of the range of techniques and the advantages and disadvantages of some of them. For instance, what ways are there for using the layout of the page to reveal the structure of the arguments being noted? What uses can be made of upper- and lower-case letters; indentations; underlining?

In all this the Tutor will not be speaking as a subject specialist, and will have, paradoxically, the *advantage* of not knowing the subject content. She will be able to approach the range of assignments with something of the same perspective as the tutee, and will sharpen comparisons between the stages of different assignments.

Wider study skills include organising time, planning appropriate questions to ask when unsure or baffled, recording ideas and facts that need to be to hand, learning to remember what needs to be remembered, and reacting appropriately to assessment and real assignment requirements. In the ideal school, each will be taught in context by the 'subject' teachers, but the Tutor will always have the central task of helping the tutee find a coherent approach to 'learning to learn'.

Facing criticism

Much unhappiness and many rows come from receiving criticism. Too often we meet the inappropriate reaction or over-reaction of a pupil only by would-be calming remarks or even reprimands. How can pupils learn to accept, resolve, or, more importantly, make use of criticism?

An important example is how a tutee should react if he considers a teacher has criticised unfairly. The exhortation 'Don't answer back' echoes often in the memory of us all, and how often it springs to our mouths. The Tutor will help members of his group to accept that in all parts of their life – in school, outside, now, and in the future – there is the risk, indeed the likelihood, of their being wrongly or partly wrongly accused. The ticket collector suspiciously calling a season-holder back for scrutiny, the police officer insisting on a breathalyser test, the shopkeeper querying the money offered are mundane examples in public places. In families, children and adults are sometimes thought to have offended when in fact there has merely been a misunderstanding. A person has to negotiate these moments, and the Tutor Group is one of the laboratories in which these negotiations are experimented upon and solutions found.

The wise Tutor will prepare for such moments and not root discussion only in the retrospective examination of particular events. For instance, text, video, or anecdote can be used to help the group imagine a particular moment. The members of the group then suggest a variety of responses, considering the advantages and problems of each. Sometimes the Tutor will have presented on the board, on the overhead projector, or in a hand-out, a list of reactions. On other occasions a list can be garnered from the ideas of the group.

Such 'distanced' episodes can be approached with a fair degree of objectivity by most members of the group. The dramatisation of fiction, autobiography, or video presentation allows the kind of objective identification described so well by Brecht in his theory of the theatre, in which the actor does not 'become' the character, but 'demonstrates' it for the audience, who are not to 'identify' with the characters, but to 'consider them'. The Tutor's role in bringing narrative (whether through fiction or the moving image) into the tutorial period is somewhat like the role of the actors speaking the prologue in Brecht's play, *The Exception and the Rule*, who exhort the audience:

Observe the conduct of these people closely:
Find it estranging even if not very strange,
Hard to explain even if it is the custom
.Hard to explain even if it is the rule
Observe the smallest action, seeming simple,
With mistrust
Enquire if a thing be necessary
Especially if it is common
We particularly ask you –

When a thing continually occurs –
Not on that account to find it natural.
    (Brecht, 1954, reprinted in Marland (ed.), 1966, p. 49)

However, the real and the immediate are also required. The wise Tutor will use the inevitable episodes of school, personal, and family life to revisit the generalities with the sharply particular. A tutee will say: 'Sir, Paul didn't half get into trouble yesterday. But it wasn't fair because . . . . .!' The Tutor can then have the members of the group devise advice for Paul from their feeling for his plight and their earlier consideration of the more objective distant event.

Tutees in a group that has been working well can share how they feel when rebuked. They can discuss responses and compare them with internal feelings: 'I just smiled at him, but inside I can tell you I was real hurt, shocked. He shouldn't have said it, but I wasn't going to let him know what he'd done to me inside!'

By talking through the reactions of characters in fiction (for instance, *LTR* Book 2, pp. 29–31) or on a video (for instance, Leake and Robottom, pp. 42–43), tutees can relate their feelings to those of characters who, although fictional, allow a fresh response. The criticised situations of pupils in schools can be illustrated through the observation of others in fiction.

'It's not fair, Miss!'

Tutees will bring a miscellaneous range of complaints about things 'not being fair', some trivial, some downright wrong, but others accounts of real injustices. The reactive Tutor makes sympathetic noises or brushes the matter to one side, occasionally embarrassedly taking up a major problem. The proactive Tutor prepares for such occasions and uses them as they happen to enable the tutee both to avoid and to cope when necessary.

Coping with a grievance is difficult for all of us some of the time and for some people most of the time. Those who cannot handle a grievance well are faced with a bitter paradox: the less well you can solve the problem, the worse the grievance becomes! From reticent festering to loud-mouthed moaning there is a repertoire of ineffective reactions to grievance. Young people are often particularly bad at expressing a complaint acceptably and positively.

Here is another example of enabling: the Tutor can address the general question of complaints: what makes a person cross with someone in authority? How can that complaint best be put? As a person being complained about, how would you feel if the aggrieved person put things in this way or that way? Many pupils feel furious impotence if a teacher has in their view been 'unfair', but they let the matter rankle, and would not know how to do otherwise.

Through discussion the Tutor will help the tutee to imagine the other person's state of mind, and consider objectively how that person would hear and see possible reactions. For instance, what are the different effects on a person of sentences starting:

'That's not fair!'
'I didn't do what you said I did yesterday.'
'You always pick on me!'
'Excuse me, Miss, could you please reconsider what you said yesterday?'
'I am sorry about yesterday, Sir, and I wonder if you have time for me to explain how I think it happened.'

One Tutor asked his tutees to think of a really complicated and difficult situation over which they felt they had been unfairly treated. They then discussed what sort of letter they could send to the allegedly unfair teacher. What would be the best opening? What is the point of the conventional courtesies and the standard salutation ('Dear Mr Smith') when you are cross? For how much should you apologize, if at all? What are you asking to be done about the event? And so on . . . . (*LTR* Book 3 has an example on p. 118.)

The Tutor is helping the tutees find a way ahead after difficulties, and thus move the role from sympathy to support for the future.

Of the many aspects of behaviour for which Tutors are responsible the way in which tutees respond to the peer-group jibes of the playground or the classroom and corridor complaints of teachers (to take just two from the range) will result from how teachers in general and Tutors in particular have prepared them for these challenges.

My argument, then, is that how tutees respond to criticism is an artefact of how the school, and within that the pastoral team, has responded to and looked after its new tutees: the Tutor can enable the tutee to make a constructive response.

The study of behaviour

From five to sixteen school life echoes family life in the frequency of admonition especially about behaviour: 'Don't' is at its most frequent in adult discourse to children. Teachers find themselves telling pupils the ways in which their behaviour was wrong and less often giving precepts about the future. Tutors are frequently cast in the role of 'Admonisher-in-chief'. To what extent does this flow of criticism of behaviour enable the tutee to take control of her behaviour? Could a Tutor in the tutorial programme teach more *about* behaviour, its causes, its effects, and how to adapt it?

Some people have feared that a consideration of 'behaviour' would be to reduce humanity to the role-performing of the procedures of external etiquette. Many of us have memories of a repeated adult instigation to 'speak nicely', 'don't do that', 'say "please"', and so on. Many teachers would see any tutorial concentration on behaviour as just more of that.

Interestingly, there is clear evidence of a relationship between maladjustment and modes of expressing emotion. My view is that one of the unfairnesses of schooling is that some pupils come into a school with an 'off-putting' style, much of which comes from the inappropriateness of their vocal tone or facial expression. Of course, there will be times when displeasing emotions have been generated and expressed. Then it is perhaps appropriate to show them and expect the reactions those emotions usually trigger. Even then, most of us would counsel some limitation of the outward expression in the interest of working towards a positive resolution of the dispute. The tutorial question is:

Does this tutee realise what he is expressing?
Does she realise what effect that expression is having on others?

In other words, is the tutee sufficiently self-conscious and self-controlling?

Many psychologists in the 1970s considered 'the child as an intuitive psychologist' (Taylor and Harris, 1984, p. 141). They scrutinised those aspects of personality that affect so much and which we normally talk about only loosely: 'the child's knowledge of memory processes and rules for self-control'. Not surprisingly, it was shown that:

Younger children know a good deal about the links between situations and the emotional reactions that they elicit. However, in contrast to children of ten years or more, they are less aware of the inner mental component to emotion, and of the possible conflict that can arise when one emotion is felt internally but another is displayed externally.

(Ibid.)

One facet of the tutorial programme should make conscious the continuation of this growth:

- 'How do people often look if . . . .?'
- 'What do other people think if someone comes into a room with *this* expression?'
- 'Which of these facial expressions (selected from a range of photographs) would you display if a teacher accused you of rudeness when you hadn't said anything?'

It is interesting that the normal increase of understanding and the use of 'control strategies' as children get older was not the case for maladjusted boys in an investigation. The following report shows the possible intervention strategy; 'prompts' help the less socially adjusted. Could not the tutorial programme help all develop their understanding and control?

The results indicate that normal and maladjusted boys differ in the strategies they propose for reacting to provocation but not in the emotion that they expect to feel. It is tempting to conclude that maladjusted boys lack knowledge of control strategies. However, it could also be argued that while they know of such strategies, they find them difficult to apply in practice or chose to adopt counteraggression instead. Indeed, it is noteworthy that slightly more than half of the maladjusted boys who failed to offer a control strategy spontaneously did offer one in reply to the experimenter's prompt.

(Op. cit., p. 144)

There is also a fair body of research evidence to support the 'commonsensical' view that the effects of young people's own behaviour affects other people's responses to them — and that in turn affects the future behaviour of those young people. 'Oppositional children elicit different types of behaviour than do passive compliant children . . . Aggressive boys tend to elicit negative behaviour from their peers' (Rutter, 1989, p. 41). The Tutor can enable tutees to understand and influence this by their behaviour.

Bullying

A variety of forms of bullying, which includes racial and sexual harassment, is prevalent in schools as it is in other groupings in society. Just as events and studies in the mid-eighties showed a much higher rate of child abuse in homes than had commonly been assumed, so studies have shown a higher incidence of bullying in schools than most of us had accepted. There are not sufficient research studies for methodical response, but sufficient for alarm (see Tattum and Lane, 1988, Chapters 1 and 2). For instance, in one small comprehensive school in which the staff did not believe bullying was a major problem, researchers (Arora and Thompson, 1987) found:

50 per cent of 14-year-olds reported that someone had tried to kick them at least once during the previous week and 36 per cent of the same group indicated that someone had

tried to break something that belonged to them. Most disturbing, all groups reported extortion – 19 per cent of 12-year-old boys presenting the highest figure.

(Op. cit., p. 9)

The studies commissioned after the murder of a boy at a Manchester school (Kelly and Cohn, 1988) showed the extent of racial name-calling and fighting – much of it hidden from teachers' perceptions. The Commission of Racial Equality's study (CRE, 1988) is similarly convincing.

Every teacher will intervene when she sees evidence, stop the trouble, and reprimand the pupils who appear to be the aggressors. Tutors who hear of one of their tutees being bullied will also be sympathetic and supportive to the victim. However, such reactions are necessary but not sufficient: they attempt to cope with the immediate needs but are not 'educational', that is they offer little opportunity for bully or victim to learn for the future. This is the work of a police officer untangling a traffic offence, not an educator.

The Tutor, of course, should not work in isolation over bullying, and the contribution of the Tutor Group should be one component in a whole-school policy, which would include:

- the school ethos and atmosphere;
- inter-staff and staff–pupil relationships;
- supervisory systems, with special emphasis on the dangerous times (dinner break and after school) and places (toilets and back corridors);
- a behaviour code devised by students, staff, and parents;
- a proper consideration of language, including how it carries association and offence;
- an anti-racist policy;
- a programme for individual and school esteem-building.

With or without such an ideal, interlocking, whole-school policy, the Tutor can make the major contribution to enable both the potential bully and potential victim to alter their behaviour. Overall it could be said that there are two forces affecting the level and intensity of bullying: the environment, social and architectural, working inwards; the inner psychology of victim and bully, working outwards.

Whilst bullying is clearly 'pathological' behaviour, its frequency makes it difficult to call it firmly 'deviant' behaviour. The danger is that considerations of the undoubted fact that, as the saying goes, 'bullying obviously meets a need' could appear to legitimise it. The Tutor's aim is to try to speculate what needs are being serviced by unpleasant behaviour and ask how those needs can be 'serviced' by non-pathological means.

In working from exhortation against bullying to enabling the tutees to reduce or remove it, Tutors will need to work from these directions:

1 How can the group help?

In probably the best essay on the school and bullying, Graham Herbert describes 'A Whole-Curriculum Approach to Bullying' and concludes with the emphasis on mobilising the peer group:

> Perhaps the most important factor in combating bullying is the social pressure brought to bear by the peer group rather than the condemnation of individual bullies by someone in authority.
>
> (Herbert, 1988, p. 82)

This is a clear example of working away from more exhortation. I have seen a Tutor Group imagine that a new pupil joins the group and finds older pupils from other groups being beastly to him. 'How', asked the Tutor, 'would you respond to seeing this happen?'

A Tutor can use the group coherence and initial support that he has engendered to enable the group to develop its dislike of and refusal to accept bullying.

2 What is bullying?

Although children have used the word since they first spoke, and 'You bully!' is a frequent phrase, it will be rare for them to have analysed bullying disinterestedly, and separately from an event, as they are asked in, for example, Science, History, or English Literature to define and analyse cause and effect, and consider strategies of response. Ideally, questions of violence and power that are in timetabled subjects, especially Social Studies, Literature, Media Studies, and Drama, should be related by those subject teachers to individuals. However, it is the Tutor's task to bring all aspects together and help the tutees see what is happening behind the show of violence.

In my view it would be ideal if the offensiveness of offensive language was analysed by linguistic experts in 'English' or 'Languages'. Instead of adults baldly and repetitively admonishing children not to use 'bad language', pupils should be helped to understand. For instance, what does 'hussy' mean and how has it come to have that meaning? Why are there so many more words to name a female judged to be promiscuous than a male, sixty-eight to nine in a current slang thesaurus (Green, 1988, p. 123)? Why is 'Paki' offensive when 'Pakistani' is appropriately descriptive? The Tutor's task, then, is to focus objectively on the language of the group and enable them to face up to the casual use of offensive vocabulary and its effects. The Tutor can help a group towards a policy of its own. This is particularly important about racist or sexist abuse. Pupils are empowered by knowledge, by realising they can adjust their vocabulary. The admonition 'control yourself' has good sense in it, but is empty unless the Tutor has empowered the tutee with the means to do it.

3 Assertiveness and life skills

It is dangerously tempting sometimes to blame the victim: 'Why did he act like that?' Whilst avoiding this, though, the Tutor should not ignore the possibility of enabling the tutees to develop fresh skills of communication to fend off the potential difficulty. These include controlling facial expression, body language, tone of voice, and style of language. This is in essence 'assertiveness training', a much misunderstood term in some jocular staffroom conversations, which suggests it is designed to make people more aggressive. In fact it does the opposite: assertiveness development enables a person to make their point, reject the unpleasant, and avoid being hurt without being aggressive. The Tutor, with the group as a whole and in individual counselling, will help tutees consider how their manner can help them keep their end up. For instance, the page opposite is material for the Tutor from *LTR* Book 1 (p. 79).

4 Understanding and practising skills

It is possible to practise ways of speaking. I have asked a group to think in their minds how they would say, for instance, 'That's not true' if they were (a) angry; (b) bored; (c) confident. After each tutee said the words, the rest of the

UNFRIENDLY PEOPLE

Trevor and the bullies

Trevor had quite enjoyed coming to the big school. Some of his friends from primary school were in the same Tutor Group and he liked that. But what Trevor didn't like was two boys from the third year. Whenever they saw Trevor they would yell out things at him, like, 'Those are smart trousers – been down the charity shop?'

This got Trevor very annoyed, because he knew that mum didn't have much money since dad had gone, and he was proud of the way his mum was dealing with everything.

At first Trevor used to fly off the handle at the two third-year boys, and he'd shout things back. Next they'd chase him and he'd have to run really fast.

Then Trevor learned to do something else when the two boys yelled out things.

▷ What else could Trevor do?
- get his friends involved?
- shout worse thing back?
- hide from the two boys?
- keep practising his running?
- worry his mum to get different clothes?
- tell his form tutor?

Talk to your neighbour about what you would do.

Here's what Trevor did:

He talked it over with people he trusted, and practised a new way of dealing with the boys. When they called out about his clothes, Trevor said (he didn't shout), 'I don't think that's funny.' It felt very strange at first, but he practised not flying off the handle. On another occasion when he was being shouted at he just said it again – 'I don't think that's funny.'

The last Trevor saw of all this was when the two boys started to chase after him. He was frightened but kept walking along in an ordinary way. The two boys decided Trevor was a bore nowadays. But Trevor's friends knew different.

Trevor learned:

Say something calmly.
Say it again.
Don't make yourself into fun for others.

Longman Tutorial Resources Book 1, p. 79

73

group put their hands up to show which tone they thought was *intended*. Of course, some speakers gave an impression other than the one they intended. How did they give the wrong impression? How could it be changed? I should say, from extensive observation and many drama lessons, secondary pupils appear to show less control over their voices than they do over their facial expressions. They can, for instance, answer a straightforward question with a tone of voice that inadvertently suggests 'what a stupid question!' But they can be helped to listen to each other and to themselves and to shape their voice to their intention. This, of course, is part of most aspects of their handling of their lives, but is also crucial to having the greatest chance of avoiding being bullied.

5 The bully himself

If a potential or actual bully is in your Tutor Group, it is unlikely that you will want to handle all aspects yourself: you will no doubt wish to consult with your team-leader. In the context of this chapter, 'From exhortation to enabling', the Tutor's task is to endeavour to help the tutee to (a) know what he is doing; (b) understand the effects of what he is doing; (c) speculate why – the hardest task; (d) speculate on the outcome, for himself now and as the year goes by; (e) ask himself if he wants to change and if he can.

The whole-group work should help all the tutees ask these questions of themselves, and the group exploration should especially help the at-risk or active bully. It will need to be supplemented by very carefully and sensitively handled one-to-one discussion in the hope of gaining further trust and assisting further self-understanding. There should also be attempts to seek the answer to the underlying question: 'What needs is this behaviour illegitimately meeting?', and then some attempt made to help the bully meet those needs in a more positive, pleasing, and self-enhancing way. Can the Tutor enable the 'bully' to make school more rewarding?

I am suggesting, then, that the frequent issue of bullying, both for aggressor and victim, is another example of how a Tutor can complement on-the-spot reaction by a deeper enabling and empowering of the tutee.

* * * * * * *

The key aspects of these explorations are obvious: the Tutor can take the initiative by finding ways of enabling the group and the individuals to find ways to an understanding of self and others and of social pressures, and through that to deciding to, and being able to, take control of self.

Much tutoring is signalling the ordinary choices made in school as a paradigm of life. The mutually respecting group led by the sensitive but intellectually clear Tutor will move from the present to the presented, from the small to the large, and from the particular to the general. Overall, the Tutor will enable the members of the group to develop their own ideas and strategies. Exhortations will fall away as the tutee is enabled to find strategies. This enabling cannot be left to the serendipity of the daily happenings, but has to be planned. This is the 'curriculum' aspect of pastoral care in general and within that, tutoring, and it is out of that planning that the 'tutorial programme' is devised – the subject of the next chapter.

5 The tutorial programme

Tutoring and the curriculum

The main formal device to seize the pastoral initiative and move from reaction to preparation is what I call 'the tutorial programme'. I mean by this the sequence of 'topics' or activities that embodies the intended learning outcomes for personal and social growth that has been agreed to be the responsibility of Tutors. Other people use other names, such as 'active tutorial work' or even 'the pastoral curriculum' (which I suggest is a misnomer, see p. 80). Indeed, some schools have no overall plan, and serendipity rules.

At one of the many moments when the country was worried about 'discipline', the government set up an enquiry, and its report summed up the basic minimum of a tutorial programme:

> Tutor periods are valuable opportunities to carry out pastoral work. They can be used to teach study skills or to deliver part of the school's PSE programme. We have emphasised form tutors' central role in effective pastoral systems earlier in this chapter. A structured programme of activities should help to develop the relationship between tutors and their groups. We recommend that secondary headteachers and teachers should identify clear aims for

the use of tutorial time, and that these aims should include reinforcing the school's behaviour policy.

(Committee of Enquiry, 1989, p. 113)

This can be seen as the minimum requirement of a tutorial programme.

It is interesting to look back to see how the positive, programmed use of tutorial time developed: on the one hand there was the sheer guilt at the waste of time (cf. Blackburn, 1975, 1983; Hamblin, 1986; Bulman, 1988; and Marland, 1981). More positively, as pastoral care moved from reactive to proactive and from hoping to help only individually to whole-group work, positive arguments were advanced for the value of the curriculum content of tutorial periods. Essentially, the argument was that pastoral care is based on personal growth, and that the growing adolescent needs to develop a range of concepts (sometimes called understanding), attitudes, facts, and skills if she is to make best use of school, develop her own sense of self, grow towards a moral understanding, es-tablish a range of social relationships, be prepared to contribute positively to community life, and be prepared for vocational choice.

To meet the students' needs we have to complement and lay foundations for individual pastoral care, and help the pupils gain the concepts, skills, attitudes, and facts likely to be required for much of their personal and social develop-ment. For this there have to be parts of the overall curri-culum which are included especially to assist these aspects of the pupil's growth. That is, parts of the curriculum have to be included primarily with a *pastoral* function – which can therefore be called 'the pastoral curriculum'. Without cur-riculum foundations, guidance is inevitably weak. For instance, how can careers officers help a student decide 'what he wants to be' when that student doesn't know what there is to be? Or how can a Tutor help a student cope better with her work if that student has no grasp of study skills? Or with racial prejudice with no consideration of ethnicity?

Obviously, many subjects have traditionally included aspects in their curriculum designed to help the pupils' personal growth: one thinks of some literature passages or some aspects of biology. However, in most schools these have been unco-ordinated offerings, separately taught in well-meaning but isolated departments. The phrase 'pastoral curriculum' (a phrase used first in my essay of 1981) implies that the school should plan whole-school approaches, and work out detailed curriculum schemes, which will then be implemented in a planned way in agreed subjects and group tutorial sessions. Thus, aspects of study skills can be taught in a planned way in the tutorial programme, Science, English, Home Economics, CDT, and Humanities.

Perhaps the most common label for this aspect of a school's work is 'personal and social education', and there is now formal inclusion of this aspect in the National Curriculum and by HMI (HMI, 1989).

When the National Curriculum was first described, many teachers thought this would erode personal and social education, and this fear lingers. However, it has been made quite clear that this is not so. Indeed, never before has 'the pastoral curriculum' been so encouraged. The Home Secretary gave a clear description of its relationship to the school as a whole:

> Personal and social education does not necessarily need to be treated as a subject in its own right. It should pervade the curriculum, not be thrust into some tiny, timetabled ghetto of its own. Personal and social education should be, in many schools already is, an integral part of school life

– in form tutorials, general studies periods or taught through the mainstream academic subjects.

(Hurd, 1988)

Whilst it is true that all aspects of a school and all its curriculum should contribute to personal and social development, there needs to be a specific whole-school policy, which I call 'the pastoral curriculum', which lists all the concepts, attitudes, facts, and skills necessary for personal and social growth.

A Tutor can think of the inter-relationship of pastoral care and the curriculum in this Venn diagram:

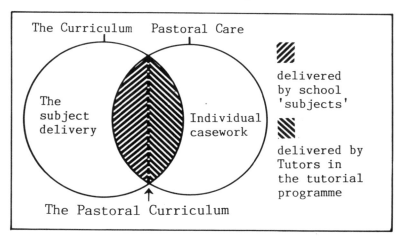

The circle on the left is the curriculum as a whole. The circle on the right is all aspects of pastoral care. The intersection (shaded) is those aspects of the curriculum required primarily and centrally for pastoral care: *the pastoral curriculum.*

Some parts of that will be 'delivered' through the 'subjects' of the school timetable, that is the curriculum divisions delivered separately. Some part will be the responsibility of

Tutors – that is, *The Tutorial Programme*. Linking everything together will be the 'cross-curricular themes' of the National Curriculum.

Ideally, these aspects of the pastoral curriculum should be clearly defined and located for 'delivery' up the years and across the teaching/tutorial organisation of the school.

Thus the tutorial programme is the planned sequence of aspects of the pastoral curriculum agreed to be the responsibility of the Tutor, closely related to his central task of enabling the tutee to understand herself and society. (Some schools and LEAs use the phrase 'the pastoral curriculum' for this. I prefer to use that phrase for *all* aspects of the curriculum related to personal and social growth. For the best analysis of 'the pastoral curriculum' see Bulman and Jenkins, 1988, and also Marland, 1981).

Clearly, some aspects of the overall pastoral curriculum will, ideally, be in both 'subject' syllabuses and 'the tutorial programme'. Guidance and support of the most individual kind depends on facts, understanding, and skills. There are properly times across the curriculum when facts and concepts are paramount and self-reflection less important – but one never completely abandons the other. I find it helpful to see the relationship in tutorial work of knowledge about self and personal skills on the one hand and facts and concepts on the other as interrelated as in this wedge diagram:

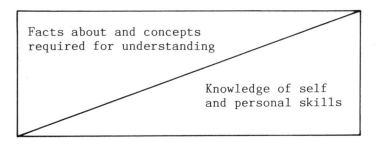

Facts about and concepts required for understanding

Knowledge of self and personal skills

The diagram is intended to indicate that it is only extremely rarely that self-understanding can be explored without some objective facts, and, conversely, it is impossible to consider facts objectively without some feeling for self-understanding: one is rarely present without the other, but the balance varies. Of course, the 'subject' syllabus part of the curriculum is presumed to lie towards the left of the diagram, and the tutorial towards the right. Both are necessary and one cannot do without the other.

It is interesting to note the difference in learning context between the two and the implications for the experience of the pupils:

- In subject periods the *personal* aspect of a topic is usually less the focus than its place in the overall structure of the subject.
- In tutorial periods the context is one in which family and home background, previous educational history, and the whole pattern of study over the week should all be well known to the Tutor. The Tutor is the main contact with home; has the greatest disciplinary influence; probably has the most intimate relationship; and above all has the broadest responsibility for the pupil's 'personal, educational and vocational guidance'. Thus topics have a different flavour, impact, and response in a tutorial period. For instance, the tutorial context for aspects of study skills has a generalising possibility less easy in a subject; discussion about relationships at home has a personal context from the Tutor's knowledge of parents and guardians less possible in Home Studies; aspects of sexuality more readily relate to the emotional than the biological in a tutorial period than in Science; anti-racism in English is looked at through language and literature, but with the Tutor also through known personal incidents; and so on.

There is a sense in which the tutorial programme merges with 'subject teaching', that is when there is a content of some form to be learned, and 'individual guidance', when the task is to respond to the pupil's personal needs. A tutorial period has to be structured like any 'lesson', but often the pupils themselves, what is happening to them or could be, is the main 'content'. Thus school events, the experiences of individual pupils, or public events can be used fully. This range is 'the tutorial programme'.

There is a reciprocal relationship between the academic subjects and the pastoral curriculum or personal and social education. HMI put it interestingly and powerfully:

> The fostering of personal and social development is a means as well as an end of education. For effective learning to occur schools have to develop a moral framework acceptable to parents, teachers and pupils within which initiative, responsibility and sound relationships can flourish. Equally, the promotion of knowledge, understanding and related competencies should contribute to the development in pupils of relevant personal, social and moral characteristics.
>
> (HMI, 1989, p. 2)

The PSE aspect of the National Curriculum, possibly together with some other of its 'cross curriculum themes' or 'issues' (known in Scotland as 'permeating elements' as 'they tend to permeate the curriculum rather than appear as discrete entities' (Consultative Committee on the Curriculum, 1987, p. 5)), can be seen as deriving from the generic description of pastoral care: 'personal, educational, and vocational guidance'. Indeed, some people call this 'the guidance curriculum'. Many schools have well-developed curriculum policies which include the pastoral curriculum (or personal and social education) facet, but you may be working in a school which has not been able to achieve this. Nevertheless, there should be some overall tutorial plan. Some schools have not yet been able to achieve this either.

The ideal tutorial programme should be a sub-set of the overall pastoral curriculum. If this has not been possible in your school, you still have the need as a Tutor to have a tutorial programme which can offer you an over-arching scheme and materials for your whole-group tutoring.

The uses of source material

Tutorial work cannot be derived entirely from the thoughts of Tutor and tutee or the actions and experiences of the group members, but needs to draw on wider source materials for a variety of purposes:

1 to set out information;
2 to 'distance' or objectify what is being discussed;
3 to evoke with the vividness of art a mood or situation;
4 to provide case studies of situations beyond those experienced directly by the members of the group.

From one point of view, the art of group tutoring is that of taking tutees away from themselves to consider aspects of relationships and then bringing them back to relate their perceptions of the other to themselves. Neither extreme is sufficient: group tutorial work cannot focus only on the tutees themselves the whole time; conversely, it cannot be looking 'out there' and away from the tutees for too long.

This moving from the immediate self to the more objective distant example and back again widens the tutees' appreciation of what people are like, and at the same time gives them deeper insight into themselves. To some extent it is the stuff of many Literature lessons, of course. However, there the text is there for its own sake and the search within oneself for points of contact is to help construct a fuller meaning of the literary work. In the tutorial session the teacher's art is reversed: the extension and reverberations of the text are there to help the tutee review himself and reconstruct her view of herself.

The kinds of source material which can be used include:

photographs
cartoons
drawings and paintings
biography and autobiography
literature
statistics
argumentative writing
factual studies.

These can be presented in a variety of formats:

printed text
wall displays
projected slides
computer programmes
work sheets
separately printed photographs
audio tapes or disc
video tapes
films
Tutor or tutee readings.

These can be grouped in a variety of ways – by their content, or their use. The important point is that the Tutor has to be willing to deploy a full range, both because of the variety of content thus explored and because of the variety of presentation for the Tutor Group.

It is wise to try to avoid a monotonous pattern of the same

sequence: stimulus/discussion/writing, though it is very easy to slip into such a routine. Tutors with different subject backgrounds will be more familiar with some formats than others – few teachers of English have used slides, few CDT teachers have used much text. However, there is nothing beyond the teacher's ordinary skill in weaving any of these forms into a tutorial session, and Tutors should be encouraged to try all.

The different kinds of stimulus material have their characteristic qualities: literature, statistics, visual images, and factual analysis explore and evoke reality in different ways. All are useful in tutorial work, but they require a self-consciously different approach. They need to be 'read' differently.

Tutors not used to discussing literature need not feel daunted by their evocation of people in particular situations. It is often helpful to read such a passage aloud to the group, as the Tutor's reading brings the characters and atmosphere to life. Sometimes a member of the group can be asked to read an extract, but it will often be wise to ask in advance so that the tutee can prepare the passage: the point of the use of the extracts is not as a reading exercise, and the aim must be to focus on the theme and thus the tutee's experience and review of self.

In general, with fiction pupils tend to be good at recalling a story sequence, naming people, and locating the events in places. However, they are often far less comfortable recalling qualitive aspects, and have even more trouble deducing the author's intentions or the extract's theme. Indeed, the distinction between 'story' and 'theme' can be very difficult for most pupils. 'It is about . . .' will lead them more often into re-telling plot than exploring theme.

Real-life descriptions or dialogues from autobiographies or news-stories can evoke powerfully situations which ring true to the tutees and clearly relate to their own understanding, but at the same time give them a fresh perspective. Audio cassettes, though not often used, are remarkably effective: there is a concentration on the experience of the words which can be lost in the visual fascination of video. (A good source is the BBC radio's *Tutorial Tasters*.) In questions and discussions the aim should be to help the members of the group participate in the thoughts and feelings of the speakers, but at the same time look at those experiences almost clinically. What is this person feeling and why? How has she come to make this decision? What would be the outcome if . . .?

Dramatised incidents can be very richly effective. The BBC's *Tutorial Topics*, for instance, takes typical school incidents, uses pupils as cast, and keeps the flavour of a real school. Alison Leake and John Robottom have devised a pupils' book to go with these episodes (Leake and Robottom, 1988). For older students the BBC's *Scene* series, although devised for English lessons, is a topic-based series of episodes, many of which enrich tutor periods.

The still photograph may strike some as less promising, but the thoughtful contemplation of a good camera portrait can be used by the skilful Tutor to quicken and deepen the tutees' understanding of self and others. The example on page 87 shows the kind of picture that can be used and gives examples of questioning techniques.

Whereas the special value of literature, biography, the media, and photographs is their power of involving the tutee, the special value of objective analysis is the complementary one of allowing breadth of consideration. The tutee is helped to stand back from considering *this* person or *that* moment and ponder more generally on how people appear to be. For instance, an obvious part of all tutorial work is to discuss gender – what is it to be a girl or boy? This could hardly be contemplated without using the vividness of art, but also the

(a) What do you think is happening here?
(b) What can you tell about the two people's feelings and thoughts from the expressions on their faces?
(c) What do you imagine the person on the right might be saying?
(d) If you were the person on the right and had just been wrongly accused of shoplifting, what would you say to the police officer?
(e) If you were the police officer and had been called by the shop manager and told that the person on the right had stolen something, how would you speak to her?

An example of the use of photographs

perspective of the social scientist and the psychologist should be used. The example on pages 90 and 91 shows how the objectivity of the psychologist can be used by a Tutor.

In all examples, Tutors should encourage tutees to be clear about the kind of material they are considering and, albeit briefly, the provenance. For instance, photographs are not 'real life' but someone's deliberate selection of a viewpoint:

Why was *this* photographed?
Why this angle?
Why is the photograph cropped as it is?
Why did the editor choose it?

Again, quotations from pupils in other schools are interesting. How do these 'real' statements differ from extracts from fiction stories? In all examples of newspaper clippings, video recordings, and audio recordings, the group should be used to 'critiquing' the material with some understanding of the mechanics of the media as recommended by the National Curriculum Council. In some schools, this training will be part of an English or arts course, or there may, though rarely, even be a special media course. However, even if there is not, the Tutor should not feel daunted by lack of specialised knowledge. An adult commonsensical approach is sufficient to help tutees question for themselves:

'To what extent can we trust this newspaper account?'
'Could the accident victim's relatives have really said this?'

And so on.

Many tutorial teams have devised their own programmes of materials, duplicated in-house. Others will be using published material. This book is part of a range of material which makes up the Longman Tutorial Resources. Experience in many schools has shown that when Tutors are first given printed material to use in tutor-group periods, many feel tied to it in a passive way that they would think quite inappropriate for learning material in their own specialist subject. This is not surprising – subject teachers have been trained so that they usually feel confident with most of their subject matter and so can use the teaching material with confidence. This often means using it flexibly, swapping, adding, deleting, or changing the order. Tutors, on the other hand, often do not have the same confidence. They will find it gradually easier as they become more experienced with whole-group tutorial work. The resources provided for tutor periods are to facilitate that work, not to dominate it. The real 'programme' is the learning aims behind the material. In no school activity should the work be limited to or by the available material.

Even those Tutors in schools using fully worked-out schemes will, of course, want to use a variety of other material, for instance:

school events
incidents in the lives of tutees
items from local newspapers
events from the national news
anniversaries and religious festivals.

Whilst it would be unwise to let a Tutor Group fall from one recent incident to the next, being responsive to events only, it would be entirely against the experiential learning of a Tutor Group not to focus on what is happening to members here and now.

Sometimes a scheme will be set aside to consider other relevant themes and at other times such supplementary material can be used to give a local context to a unit in the main schemes. For instance, a Tutor using 'Division of labour in the home' from *LTR* Book 3 (p. 17) might use a clipping from a national newspaper; a Tutor using

Boys and girls: any real differences?

Lots of girls think that other girls make the best friends.

Lots of boys think that other boys make the best friends.

Some girls and boys think you can be good friends with the opposite sex too.

It can all depend on whether or not you think girls and boys are really different.

Do you think that certain sorts of attitudes and feelings, certain abilities and kinds of behaviour, go with being a girl and being a boy?

What do you expect?

If you visited the homes of your friends, are there any jobs that you wouldn't expect women or men to carry out there?

On a piece of paper, write M for male or F for female or B for both after considering the jobs listed below:

- changing plugs
- carrying out the kitchen rubbish
- changing a baby's nappy
- paying the electricity bill
- washing up
- feeding the baby
- sending notes to school
- doing the shopping

Are there any real differences between baby girls and boys?

Do you think there are many differences between newly born baby girls and boys other than their genitals?

One of the chemicals in the body that leads to differences between males and females is called 'testosterone'. A study of the actual

measurements of testosterone in a large sample of newly born baby girls and boys shows something unexpected about the difference in testosterone levels.

Look at the graph below: what does it tell you about the difference between the testosterone levels for boys and girls in the blood of newly born babies?

The graph and the tests on this page were researched by Professor Carol Jacklin.

ASSIGNMENTS ▷ ▷ ▷ ▷ ▷ ▷ ▷ ▷

1 With a partner, can you think of ways in which adults start teaching young children what is expected of girls and what is expected of boys?

2 Looking back to your primary school, can you think of any ways in which the teachers treated boys and girls differently?

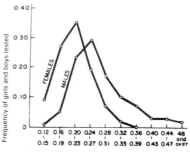

Testosterone concentrations (ng/ml) in new-born babies

Who's stronger?

The questions below are to help you think whether there are any differences between girls and boys at birth, and to try to assess how important any differences are.
Write your answers on a separate piece of paper and check them with your tutor when you've finished.

Doctors tried sixty different tests to find differences in behaviour between girls and boys in the first few days after birth (such as looking at how they reacted when touched, finding out whether they could turn their heads). Do you think differences in behaviour were found regularly between the baby girls and boys:
– with every test?
– with one half of the tests?
– with a quarter?
– with one fifth?
– with none of them?

Measurements were taken of the ability of very young babies to lift their heads when lying down. Do you think:
– more girls than boys could lift their heads highest and longest?
– more boys than girls could lift their heads highest and longest?
– about the same number of boys and girls could lift their heads highest and longest?

The strength of the baby's grip was also measured. Do you think:
– the strength of the grip was greatest in girls?
– it was greatest in boys?
– it was equal between them?

The strength and frequency of movements was tested and counted. Do you think:
– there were more and stronger movements from boys?
– there were more and stronger movements from girls?
– the movements were about the same for both sexes?

Mothers and fathers were asked to describe the physical characteristics of their babies soon after birth. The fathers had not held their babies, but only looked at them through a window. They described their daughters as small and delicate but their boys as strong and big. Do you think:
– the fathers were right when the descriptions were checked against actual measurements?
– they were wrong?
– they were about half right in each case?

And do you think mothers who had held their babies and fed them were more or less likely to be right than the fathers?

When you've checked your answers, compare them with those of the rest of the Tutor Group.
In your opinion which statement is correct?
– At birth, girls are stronger than boys.
– At birth, boys are stronger than girls.
– At birth, girls and boys are equally strong.

In small groups, think about the questions on the next page.

'Homework' from Book 1 (p. 32) would obviously use the school's own procedures.

Much tutorial work has had ambitions beyond the available material, and Tutors have been improvising too extensively. In these groups anecdote, opinion, and garrulous talk about little have led to shallowness. Other schools have replaced the boredom and emptiness of listening with the boredom of toying with a worksheet that demands action but not thought. Successful group tutoring requires the flexible use of a wide range of source material to inform, evoke, stimulate and prompt.

There is an interesting contrast between the use of a piece of literature or a drama video, say, in a tutor session and in an English lesson. For instance, the BBC's *Tutorial Topics* (Leake and Robottom, 1988) includes a dramatised presentation of a bullying incident. It is a good twenty-minute play set in a boys' school. The English teacher using such a piece would, of course, ask for memories and speculation about bullying as part of the lesson. However, those personal experiences would be evoked primarily to help the pupils react to and make sense of the drama. Conversely, the Tutor is using the drama to help the tutees make sense of their own experience.

Of course, I am exaggerating the polarity: all reading and watching drama helps the reader or audience consider their own human predicament. As Doris Lessing says of one of her characters:

> She therefore got out of bed, and went into the living room, and knelt in front of the bookcase. Books. Words. There must surely be some pattern of words which would neatly and safely cage what she felt – isolate her emotions so that she could look at them from outside. . . . And so she knelt in front of a bookcase, in driving need of the right

arrangement of words . . . with the craving thought, what does this say about my life?

(Doris Lessing, *A Proper Marriage*, MacGibbon & Kee, 1965)

However, there is some use in the polarity from the Tutor's presentational point of view: she must focus the introduction, the purpose, and the follow-up in terms of enabling the tutees the better to understand situations so that they can control themselves and the situation better. The art is there primarily to help them take a better grip on themselves and their surroundings.

The programme and the experience

Over the year there should be a reciprocal relationship between individual and whole-group tutorial programme work, with the former sometimes prompting and illuminating the latter, and in its turn the programme being called upon in individual counselling.

If the tutee is to objectivise his behaviour, he needs to be able to stand outside, as it were, and look on as a spectator. One help towards this is the provision of data on the behaviour of others.

For instance, if school attendance is being discussed, there are ample data in the school and nationally against which *this* Tutor Group's attendance pattern can be put, and against which each pupil can consider herself. Speculation about cause and effect in the behaviour of others helps towards the analysis of self. A Tutor Group of twelve- and thirteen-year-olds could be asked to consider the facts about absence and smoking habits from a large survey of children of the same age:

Numbers (percentages) of absences related to children's smoking

	Never smoked	Sometimes smoked	Regularly smoked
Boys	181/877 (21)	109/486 (22)	21/45 (47)
Girls	157/947 (17)	117/487 (24)	17/43 (40)

(Charlton and Blair, 1989, p. 91)

Why are regular smokers absent from school more often than other children? Could it be chance, an unrelated correlation? Does the smoking *lead* to absence, perhaps through ill health? Does lack of success at and interest in school lead to absence, and the absence itself lead to smoking? Or, even, as parental smoking appears to lead to less good health in children, does early ill health lead to less success in school, and so more absence?

A discussion of these hypotheses and exploration of the facts and their interpretation is well within the ideas and skills of almost all second-year secondary Tutor Groups. Indeed, give or take a few points of vocabulary and syntax, their arguments are likely to be as thoughtful, shrewd, and relevant as those of the researchers, who summed up:

Our findings suggest that children who smoke and whose parents smoke are more likely to be absent from school for minor ailments. Their schoolwork would then suffer and they might be underachievers because of their smoking and their families' smoking rather than smokers because of their underachievement. A mother's smoking during pregnancy, while breast feeding, and during a child's early infancy can cause considerable health risks to the child long before that child has started smoking. If the child thus starts school already with an increased risk of absence failure to keep up with his or her peers could begin immediately, paving the way for underachievement and a negative attitude to school early in his or her educational career and leading to an increased risk of smoking.

(Op. cit., pp. 91–2)

On the one hand, a major pressure on young people is to conform with the Tutor Group – the pressure of the peer group. On the other hand, most (though not all) young people want to 'be themselves'. Facts and understanding are required to facilitate this independence. The following matrix is an attempt to define the relationships:

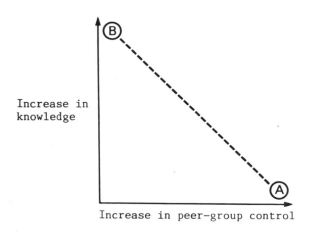

A pupil at A is under the maximum control of the peer group and has little knowledge to achieve independence. However a pupil at B is less controlled by the peer group and has a large knowledge base.

I have seen this process of using tutees' own analysis of their behaviour as a comparison with figures garnered from distant studies used most profitably. For instance, I observed a second-year secondary Tutor Group considering their watching of television. One week each tutee had noted her or his own estimate of the pattern of TV viewing over the week, totting up a typical weekly total. Then their Tutor had asked each tutee to keep a diary for the week, noting the *actual* figure of TV viewing for each night. The following week's tutorial session focused on the tabulation of the previously filed expectation against the reality. As an external referent, national television-viewing figures were then compared.

Conclusion

As a designated Tutor, you have the right to expect:

1 an overall brief on the role of a Tutor;
2 an outline of the general 'pastoral curriculum' or 'PSE programme' for the school;
3 a more detailed description of the content of the tutorial responsibility;
4 tutee learning material within and exemplifying that. This is a 'tutorial programme'.

In many schools Tutors will find that they do not have any of the components. In some others, there will be only a few. A tutorial programme is essential.

6 Relating to homes

Introduction

A school owes a duty to the homes of its pupils. Our families look to us not only to teach their children, but to relate to them as families. Further, it has become clearer than ever that when home and school work together the pupil has a greater chance of success, families are happier, and teachers have greater professional satisfaction. (See Macbeth, 1989, for an overview.) Recent research has demonstrated it, and a range of DES and HMI statements have stressed it. For instance, on discipline, the Elton Committee recommended:

> We draw attention to evidence indicating that the most effective schools tend to be those with the best relationships with parents. We urge heads and teachers to ensure that they keep parents well informed, that their schools provide a welcoming atmosphere which encourages parents to become involved, and that parents are not only told when their children are in trouble but when they have behaved particularly well.
>
> (Committee of Enquiry, 1989, p. 14)

That clearly puts a considerable emphasis on the tutorial role, and yet we appear to have considerable difficulties, and really not very much success. I estimate, for instance, that there are eight times as many family complaints about poor communication as there are criticising teaching. The Tutor is the main person for a school's relations with families, and this chapter addresses this task.

Difficulties

Even experienced teachers, sometimes to their surprise, feel considerable difficulty in working with parents. They might take some comfort from knowing how widespread this lack of confidence is. Indeed, we have hard figures from an HMI study of how new teachers feel about their preparation. 'Fewer than two in 10 new teachers felt well prepared to liaise with parents and others in the community' (HMI, 1988, p. 34). Indeed, HMI themselves found evidence of inadequate preparation:

> Comments on preparation to liaise with parents and others in the community were made in equal numbers by primary and secondary teachers. Only two mentioned having received any form of preparation and that occurred during teaching practice. Over thirty teachers were critical of their lack of training in this respect. Among the critical comments were several from teachers on the subject of parents' evenings. One was 'unsure how to conduct interviews with parents' and another was 'totally unprepared for her first parents' evening'.
>
> (Op. cit., p. 35)

It is insufficient to assume that teachers will take working with parents in their stride, especially as the hours spent with pupils in classes and with other teachers in planning and discussion take up so much time, and in even the keenest teacher's year there will only be a tiny fraction of that time working with parents. *You can be an experienced teacher and still inexperienced with your tutees' families.* An objective study of home–school relations in the European Economic Community (Macbeth, 1981) has shown the UK as having the least frequent home–school contacts. How can a Tutor move forward realistically?

Getting to know the family

The better you know a particular family's pattern, the better you will be able to relate to that family. Getting to know a family requires a very open mind: we have so many stereotypes of families that we too often jump to conclusions. It is easy to guess an entirely wrong family composition. (*LTR* Book 1 gives the facts for the UK for the tutees to consider on page 107.) It is easy to presume a pattern of family life on the basis of a few snippets of knowledge that prove quite wrong. So the first step is to avoid guessing.

Almost all secondary schools will have a file for each student, and this will include some form of record from the junior school (and previous secondary school if the pupil has transferred). Most also gather the basic family information afresh when a pupil is received into secondary school. This is best done not only by a questionnaire, but by a complementary 'reception interview'. Such an interview should ask for the key information:

the adults caring for the pupils;
their relationship to the pupil and (if more than one) to each other;
the names and titles by which they wish to be known;
if the pupil's two biological parents are not the present caring adults, how and when did the absent parent/s leave, and what is their present relationship with the pupil?

the occupations of the caring adults;
correct addresses and telephone numbers of home and work;
any siblings' names, ages, and present education or occupation;
ethnicity of family members;
languages spoken;
housing conditions in broad terms.

Over many years' experience of interviewing families, I have nearly always found families anxious to speak about themselves: the school is a privileged recipient as it enters the partnership of assisting with the education of the young person.

Whether the Tutor Group is new to the school or you are taking over an established group, it is well worth looking through those files to back up the bald details of the register. Indeed, you will not want to make simple slips like wrong names, including dead parents, or misunderstanding relationships, and you may therefore like to prepare a personal checklist. At the least, families deserve the courtesy of correct names: if your tutee is called John Frazer and his parents Mary Jones and Jack Frazer, they should not be written to as Mr and Mrs Frazer! Similarly, Islamic family name patterns should be understood and used correctly.

Making first contact

Having done your homework, a general introductory letter is a welcome and practical first step. I find that this is not very commonly done, but when done is appreciated. If your school sends out circular letters with tutor names, this may not be necessary. Even so, a letter to the parents of your

St. Agnes High School

VICTORIA ROAD NORTHWOOD HAMPSHIRE HA3 5PA   Tel. 0456 3434

Headmaster: R A Franks BA

To the families of pupils in 3Q   6th September 1992

Dear Parents or Guardians,

I know that after two years of working with him the pupils of 3Q and their parents and guardians were very sad that Mr Cheshire retired at the end of last year. You will be pleased to hear that he and his wife are happily settled in their new home – and he seems to be as active in the community as ever!

May I introduce myself as your daughter's or son's new Tutor. I have been in the school for many years now, and I know the pupils of this group rather well as I taught my subject, Mathematics, to them last year (and I shall continue teaching them this year also). Mr Cheshire has briefed me very thoroughly, and I am familiar with each pupil's records and her or his work last year.

I look forward to getting to know you also. I shall read the pupil's <u>Diaries</u> every Thursday during the morning, and I shall look out for your comments. Please keep in touch with me. You can always write a brief note in the <u>Diary</u> or send in a separate letter. In particular, please let me know if you have any suggestions, worries, or queries. I also need to know if for any reason your son or daughter is unable to be at school.

If you want to speak to me on the phone, please ask for the Lower-School staffroom. Of course, I teach most of the periods, and if I am not available please leave a message in the Lower-School office, and I shall try to phone you back as soon as possible.

I shall be looking at all the work of the pupils in my group, and especially concentrating this year on further developing their study skills – remembering that they start their two-year GCSE course next year. We shall also be starting work towards their option choices. This is very important, not only so that they choose the best subjects to add to the national curriculum and the best opportunities for them to cover the national curriculum itself, but also because this task of considering and choosing is in itself important to every pupil's personal and intellectual growth. The first meeting to hear about this will be on October 6th, and I'll send you the details later.

I am looking forward to the year's work with my new Tutor Group, and I think that they will all do very well.

Best wishes,
Yours sincerely,

Brenda Casey

Mrs Brenda Casey
Tutor of 3Q

A Tutor's introductory letter home

101

tutees introducing yourself, saying what you hope to achieve, and how you can best be contacted is very helpful. How much better that your first communication should be a warm, helpful, and pleasant one, rather than, perhaps, your first letter being an absence query! A sample letter (the school and names are fictional) is shown on page 101.

Keeping in touch

From then on, the Tutor will want to keep each tutee's family as well informed as possible. Many schools have some form of booklet which is used for regular interchange of facts – homework assignments, absences, special arrangements, and notes on good work or difficulties. Below is a page from the North Westminster *Diary*:

Week No. 1			Commencing	
Date	Subject			Remarks
Mon.				
Tues.				
Weds.				
Thurs.				
Fri.				
Tutor's Comments .... Signed .... Date .... Page 14			Parent's/Guardian's Comments .... Signed .... Date .... Page 15	

The early pages of this termly booklet give homes the names of the key teachers at school, and a page of advice to parents, translated into the main languages used by the families of the school. There is a double-page spread such as this for each week: subject teachers are expected to ensure that the defined homework assignment is copied into the appropriate space; families are expected to check that this tallies with the homework timetable set out earlier; all teachers are expected to enter comments and points of interest. Tutors are expected to oversee the communication flow, and the weekly exchange of comments between Tutor and home is the lynchpin of communication.

For such a scheme to work, the school as a whole has to be behind it and to work at the details. For instance, every subject teacher has to be meticulous about ensuring that homework assignments are noted, and praise or criticism entered. From the Tutor's point of view, such a scheme helps her to build up a picture of the tutee across the curriculum and in the school as a whole. From the family's point of view, though, this is the main link with the school, and they will see it primarily as a way of hearing from and speaking to you as a Tutor. It repays care.

If you are tutoring in a school without such a booklet, you will find both the cross-school picture and the home–school link harder to build up: to formulate every point in the form of a letter is more laborious and can be artificial over small points. Tutors without the support of a 'Diary' booklet would be well advised to devise a simple form of quick messages, something like that shown on page 104. Such a slip can be used easily and partly makes up for the lack of a booklet. (A range of other devices is discussed in Macbeth, 1989.) It

WAVERLEY SCHOOL

Station Road Bishop Norton Lancashire I A4 6PL
Telephone: 562 8864

FROM MS GRACE, TUTOR OF 2GH

Date:......................

To the parents or guardians of:................................

Please excuse this quick note, but I thought you would want to
know at once that:

I should be grateful if you could contact me by a note or phone
to let me know your reactions as soon as possible.

signed:.............................

A sample proforma note from a Tutor

would, of course, be better if an NCR copy could be kept in school, but such sophistication would put the scheme beyond the scope of a Tutor's organisation.

Letters

There will be times when a full letter is required, especially when a Tutor observes significant developments, notable achievements, problems, or examples of worrying bad behaviour. There are two obvious difficulties: shortage of time and the shortage of clerical facilities in most schools. One has to add a less often mentioned one: how rarely a school teacher has the occasion to write professionally for an adult audience. We have a tendency to be abrupt, to use pointlessly 'official' language, and to be strangely cold:

'I have to tell you . . . .'

'It has come to our attention that your son/ daughter . . . .'

'I must insist . . . .'

'It is our policy that . . . .'

The passive is over frequently used in sentences apparently afraid of the point: 'It has become clear that . . . .' Often the writer so suppresses his own voice that he sounds like a clerk working mechanically to the instructions of superiors.

Conversely, as in speaking, it is easy to let indignation or strength of feeling lead to downright insulting remarks. One pupil's father complained that his son's Tutor had said of a matter of option choice over which there was a disagreement between the Tutor and the father: 'What a pity you've chosen that when Tom is so capable. Parents are usually more caring in these matters.'

I advise that letters should as far as possible be phrased with warmth, courtesy, and hope. 'Officialese' should be banished. An appropriate introductory paragraph should normally be used, picking up the relationship where it was last left aside, as adults do in other contexts, for example:

```
Dear Mrs Brown,

I was glad to hear that your youngest daughter has settled so
well into her junior school. You must be very pleased.

When we last spoke, I promised to let you know how John seems
to be managing the range of preparation for GCSE. Although
there are still some difficulties, you will be pleased to
hear  . . . . . . . .
```

Tutor-group family meetings

Tutor-group parents' meetings are used successfully in a number of schools: the Tutor invites parents to meet each other and him. This is particularly useful early in the life of a group. An invitation, giving the expected time of ending and the main purpose, is much appreciated:

Castle Gate School

School Lane Ipswich Suffolk SO4 3DP
Telephone: 765 4370

To the parents and guardians of pupils of 4J   25th September, 1991

Dear Guardians and Parents,

As I promised you when I wrote to introduce myself at the start of the year, I have arranged for a meeting of the families of the students in my Tutor Group:

<u>Wednesday, 16th October, 6.30pm</u>

The main purpose is for parents and guardians to be able to meet me and the new Head of Year, Miss Oakes. Please bring your daughter or son if you wish. There will be coffee and biscuits at 6.30pm, and some members of the Tutor Group will be here in advance to greet you and introduce you to others.

At about 7.00pm Miss Oakes and I will give a very short description of the special features of this term, with particular reference to assessment in relation to the National Curriculum and progress towards GCSE. This will last only some twenty minutes, and then we shall be happy to answer questions about general matters until 8.00pm. I promise that no-one need stay after that, though we should both be happy to speak to families individually about personal queries if you would like to stay.

There will be a display in the room of the group work we have been doing in tutorial sessions, which I hope will interest you.

We look forward to seeing you.

Best wishes,

Yours sincerely,

Harry J Counter

Harry J. Counter
Tutor of 4J

A Tutor's invitation to a Tutor-Group parents' meeting

Whether best held in the usual tutor-group room or in a slightly larger and less desk-filled venue needs debating – both have their advantages. A cup of tea or coffee helps the start, though it is not essential. Introductions and informal talk should be allowed a little time, but fairly soon the Tutor should convene the meeting, covering, perhaps, some routine points, how the group is settling in, and the main needs. Families should then be invited to ask questions about any aspect of the school and its working. The Tutor should note and promise to follow up any problems, however small. You need to be relaxed but precise – resisting the temptation to be too defensive about the school. Parents prefer, and deserve, honesty about difficulties.

Tutor-group parent sessions can have a variety of focuses. I have described the value of an 'induction' session for a group new to the school. An end-of-year review is another possibility; pre-fourth-year option choices is a frequent example; and GCSE preparation is very valuable.

David Kibble described his use of a session on study skills for the parents of fifth-year students (Kibble, 1988). (One could argue that late in the fourth year would be even more timely.) Obviously such work with parents must relate to the tuition given to the students. David Kibble summed up:

> In discussion the parents said how valuable it had been to learn about revision techniques. Many realised how inefficient pupils might be. One parent commented that his own son had adopted some of the techniques of study and revision following the pupils' study skills course and now felt himself to be much more efficient. The father was able to see why. Here was an excellent example of the true partnership of school and parent I mentioned earlier. Other parents felt that sharing experiences and ideas had been the most valuable part of the evening. They felt that

they were more able to understand the pressure on their children and the subsequent 'distancing' and bad temper of some of their sons and daughters.

(Op. cit., p. 43)

Obviously, such events can, and perhaps should, be organised for a whole year group, but from time to time special tutor-group meetings are well worth while.

Out of this could come a Tutor Group Association, as recommended in the Hargreaves report (Hargreaves, 1984). Whether the paraphernalia of an 'Association' strengthens the home–school work of a Tutor or overburdens it with machinery is a decision each school has to make. Each parent or guardian should, though, feel 'associated' with the Tutor and the group by a range of devices and contacts.

The family and the tutor programme

Tutors should try to create an atmosphere in which their tutees know that their homes are respected and that there is mutual trust. There will be occasions (as in a family) when the Tutor will make it clear to her tutee that something (perhaps an unsatisfactory but uncharacteristic piece of behaviour) will not be passed over but will not be passed on.

There should be a conscious addressing of the matter of family care and responsibility in the whole-group tutorial programme. This is yet another instance of relating pastoral casework to the pastoral curriculum. For instance, Book 1 has a section on homework, and this requires a self-conscious consideration of home–school information and planning (*LTR* Book 1, p. 32–9). Similarly, 'School and Home' in that book (pp. 105–6) addresses the relationship directly:

SCHOOL AND HOME

School and home – how are they getting on?

Now that you've been in your first year for a while, you've got to know the school, and people in school have got to know you.

And what about the folks at home?

Have they got to know school? Has school got to know them?

• •

A fun quiz for parents/guardians

How many of these questions could they answer?

1 What's the name of your tutor?
2 What's your favourite lesson?
3 Which evening do you get Maths homework?
4 Which subject do you find most difficult?
5 How is a meeting arranged with someone at school?
6 What classes for adults does the school put on?

▷ Talk over with your neighbour the ones that you think your parents/guardians might not be able to answer.

Have they been given the answers at any time?

Now it's the school's turn

How many of these questions could your tutor answer?

1 Who are the parents/guardians/adults you live with?
2 What are their names?
3 Do you have any brothers or sisters?
4 What hobbies/activities does your family enjoy?
5 Which of your lessons are they most concerned about?
6 Who would be contacted in emergency, and how?

▷ Talk over with your neighbour the ones that you think your tutor may not be able to answer.

Has s/he been given the answers at any time?

• •

'Could do better'?

▷ Now it's your turn. You're going to write a report on school and on home, telling each of them how they could do better in doing their part toward your progress at school. You could also tell them what you think they should learn about each other.

Discuss your ideas in the Tutor Group before you deliver your reports to your tutor and your home.

Longman Tutorial Resources Book 1, p. 105

Thus the Tutor will want to help tutees think in a general way about how and why schools and homes work together so that the individual pupil can make sense of his individual experiences – and know what to expect. Indeed the tutee ought to be helped to know the *rights* that his family have in terms of school, and understand the respective duties of school and home. The third-year subject choice programme (*LTR* Book 3, pp. 45–57) are times when the relative predominance of each member of the pupil–school–home trio can be consciously addressed. In the older years the changing balance of responsibility is an issue for group discussion (see, for instance, 'An Adult in the Family', *LTR*, Book 6).

Ideally, questions of family will be addressed as part of the wider PSE whole-curriculum plans in the school. In those contexts the idea of family should be explored – what patterns are there today, in the past, and in different cultures? *LTR* Book 1 (pp. 107–11) asks the members of the group to consider their place in their family and how families work. The 'social studies' approach to family is objective and generalised, but ideally should be there to underpin tutorial work. The tutorial approach relates the understanding of family to the tutee's consideration of self: 'Who am I?' involves asking 'What is my family? How do I work with it? How does my school work with my family?'

Conclusion

No Tutor will ever regret effort, care, time, and generosity offered to the families of her tutees. There will be occasional disappointments and misunderstandings, but even for those families the Tutor will feel the happier for genuinely having tried.

At a time when the profession is under pressure and an individual's duties are being more precisely defined by the *School Teachers' Pay and Conditions Document* (DES, 1987) and its successors, it may appear ingenuous to stress the value of generosity of emotion and time to families. However, it is a privilege to be able to have a Tutor's relationship with families, and the personal rewards are very great – as is the gain for your tutee.

7 Individual casework

Introduction

Although the theme of this book is that tutoring is centrally concerned with working with and through the group, the Tutor's aim is to enable the individual to be more fully and truly her- or himself with understanding of and respect for others. Just as frustration for the Tutor and starvation for the tutee comes from a well-intentioned but essentially ill-designed and impractical attempt to offer tutorial pastoral care only through one-to-one discussion, so whole-group tutoring cannot complete the task alone.

Much of the Tutor's work requires individual, one-to-one 'counselling': very often pupils will need talking with and will benefit from a conversation with their Tutor. Such conversations, in snatched moments, after school, or in a methodically planned series of 'review' meetings, sometimes involve questioning, sometimes advising, sometimes exhorting, and often passing on ideas or facts which the pupil needs for his own decision-making. They are an essential extension of and complement to the whole-group tutoring. Indeed there is a sense in which the latter underpins or serves the former. I have described some aspects of the reciprocity in Chapter 5, pp. 76–83).

It is clearly a weakness of the UK school system that such crucial individual sessions are not budgeted for, and neither structured nor scheduled: Tutors have to find time by a variety of devious strategies.

As an LEA inspection says of one school: 'Many problems are literally dealt with in "passing"' (ILEA, 1986, p. 11). Tutors usually find that individual, semi-private talks are prompted by events, too often urgent and unhappy ones, and have to be held in awkward places: the pastoral care of the corridor! Contrast the boarding-school 'housemaster' or 'housemistress', usually with only some thirty or so pupils for whom she is personally responsible, and who has the hours of a full day to schedule, and a study for a proper meeting.

Most Tutors have always been generous with their non-scheduled time. Paradoxically, the concept of a time-ceiling, brought in by the *School Teachers' Pay and Conditions Document 1987*, can be used to help. The 'directed time' is in effect a *protected* limit. A school can build in an allocation of personal tutorial time within this overall limit. The specific budgeting of such time would appear a necessary corollary of encouraging full tutorial work. Such budgeting is both practical, because it cuts other scheduled tasks (for example, limiting class subject teaching), and symbolic, because it *states* the reality of the need for time for Tutor and tutee to meet with no competing claims: *tutoring requires Tutor and tutee to meet on their own sometimes.*

Getting to know the tutee

In essence, the first steps are the same as those I have described for the tutee's family on pages 99–100: the file is not the end nor sufficient, but it is a necessary start, too often overlooked. The shrewd Tutor will look for the euphemistic phrase from the junior school, the tell-tale worried remarks, achievements, interests, and characteristics.

Of course, there are dangers in being over-influenced by

the past: the tutee has to be allowed to have a free future. On the other hand the tutee is not a *tabula rasa*, and to erase the growth of junior school years is naive and counter-productive. 'The child is father of the man' and the continuities of growth are as strong as the discontinuities. (Interested readers will find surveys of what is known about these aspects of growth in Rutter, 1989, and Robbins and Rutter, 1989.) No Tutor would wish to judge the present or future potential of a tutee from those records of the past. On the other hand, it would be rash not to make good use of those records. It is amateur to say, 'I don't like to know too much about the pupil's past'. The professional need is to know and the professional skill is to make good use of the information. Sensitive study of the records, tempered by a refusal to label, is a vital first step.

This is equally true of the new secondary pupil (for whom a full junior-school file should be available) or the pupil being taken over 'mid-stream' (as it feels) by a secondary Tutor after one, two, or three years. In this case, the immediacy of the records and the fact that the notes, reports, or letters have been written by colleagues known to the new Tutor makes fresh judgement more difficult. The new Tutor needs to make as conscious an effort to read and listen when he takes a group over as when the pupils are new to the school.

Following the discussions with the previous Tutor (if at all possible) and the careful study of the file, a Tutor newly taking a group will want to schedule a series of personal meetings along the lines described on pages 119–20.

Looking forward

There is, though, another weakness, one which is perhaps an even deeper problem: most Tutor–tutee meetings are *retrospective*, as are most personal guidance sessions in UK secondary schools. We are doing our best to help a pupil cope with her problems *after* some difficulty, upsetting event, failure, or missed opportunity. The ratio in our tutoring of time spent mopping up trouble to time spent enabling pupils to avoid trouble and positively to make good use of opportunities is sadly unbalanced. How often do we have to talk with a pupil *after* some difficulty rather than before? How often do we find that our individual 'guidance' session willy-nilly becomes a mini-lesson, as we have to impart information required by the pupil. Our pupils sometimes face racism unprepared, choices unprepared, and each step in their schooling takes them by surprise.

My thesis is that a planned tutorial programme and whole-group tutoring are the broad, fundamental bases of pastoral care, and that these make a major contribution to shifting pastoral care from the reactive to the proactive. However, the individual work also has to have this component: to talk only after difficulties is not to make best use of talk.

Such routine 'review' meetings have the advantage of there being no recent 'problem' and none of the tension of teacher reprimanding pupil. Their disadvantage is that, lacking apparent purpose, they may appear pointless. I should advise the Tutor, therefore, to consider the following approaches:

1 Relate these scheduled review meetings to the tutorial programme, so that tutees not only know that they are coming and do not associate them (as they do most meetings with teachers) with 'trouble', but also understand their purpose.

2 Make the main format of the meetings clear in advance and especially what it would be helpful for tutees to think over in advance.

3 Structure the meeting so that the tutee can raise matters

and has space to respond personally, and also so that the talk is not merely desultory – the tutee should be conscious that major aspects of her developing pupil-ship are being covered.

4 Whenever appropriate, relate the individual discussion to aspects of the group-work and the tutorial programme. There is an educative reciprocity when tutorial-programme issues feed in as a background and, conversely, when the depth of individual Tutor–tutee discussion can be used by the tutee in group work.

Finally, such meetings ought ideally to have a summary: 'So, we are agreed that . . . .' And the tutee should feel some 'ownership' of this summary, being free to add ('But, please don't forget, Miss, that I . . . .') or contradict ('Sir, is that fair when you agreed that I did . . .?'). In the fourth and fifth years this will be part of the Record of Achievement, but the *process* should be regularly revisited from about the end of the first term. From, say, the third year the Tutor could consider giving the tutee a written copy of such a summary.

Monitoring

A plethora of signals of varying degrees of authenticity will reach a Tutor about his tutees around the school. Some of these will be contradictory, and, however good the pupil is, the majority will be critical: it is a sad fact that we find the time or energy to pass on encouraging news less often.

A Tutor will need to extend and complement this un-solicited selection of comments by specific enquiries, either as routine (for instance, as part of school reports home) or when occasion arises (such as, when considering the overall situation of an individual tutee before meeting her parents).

Some schools have standard comments sheets to circulate. Some Tutors prefer to send to their colleagues a simple note:

```
                              This copy for....................................

        Memorandum to all teachers of Leroy Foot, 4Z3

        Because of his family's worries about whether he is under-achieving and whether
        we are setting him stretching enough assignments, I am reviewing Leroy's work and
        attainment and meeting his parents on the Tuesday after half-term.

        Could you please return this slip to me with your estimate of his achievement in
        this first half term of the course. I would especially appreciate any views on
        whether he finds the work too easy and how much effort he appears to be putting
        into the work you set.

        Could you please return this by October 15th. Thank you very much!

        I will let all his teachers know the outcome of the discussion.
    ----------------------------------------------------------------------------------------
        RE: LEROY FOOT        MEMORANDUM TO MOHAMMED KASSIM, TUTOR OF 4Z3

        Subject:                                    Teacher's Name:....................




                                      Signed:
                                      Date:
```

The cumulative sequence of work in ordinary exercise books and folders is, of course, the main signalling a Tutor receives. No Tutor could review all this work regularly, but from time to time it is well worth while looking at a sample of each of your tutee's work: you do not have to be a subject expert to get something of an impression. Only the Tutor is in a position of having an overview of all the work. This is not to be missed.

The time and the place

Therefore, ideally, every Tutor needs to have bespoke time (a) for a rota of 'review' sessions, and (b) to be kept clear for booked sessions of the unplanned but not necessarily 'emergency' talks. I shall discuss each of these.

First, though, where? Although much valuable human intercourse can take place 'on the run' as two people are moving from one place to another, for a Tutor to have one of his key tasks scheduled, as it were, for corridors is clearly careless. Of course, many significant interchanges inevitably and properly arise out of whole-group sessions or recent experiences and gain in immediacy what they lose in tranquillity from a brief, 'on the spot', word:

'You seemed upset then, Omar.'

'Did you really mean to be so cutting, Tracey?'

'Leroy, I thought you were really helpful to Mary.'

. . . and so on.

The tutee rushing in at the end of the afternoon with a tale of woe from his English lesson has to be responded to. The news that is picked up during the day that a boy's sister has died, or a girl has been accused of stealing a purse, . . . all the rich pointillism of a Tutor's day, often, indeed usually, has to be responded to whilst it is still vivid. These moments will be by the door, in the corridor, in the corner of the room, or sometimes, thankfully, with the Tutor seated by her desk and the tutee by her, despite the activities of others in the room.

The unplanned will demand this awkwardness of time and location, but this is not good enough for consistent tutoring. At least, the Tutor will want to see some of his tutees when the tide of the day has ebbed away, and he can sit with the tutee in an almost quiet room.

However, the full tutor room is not ideal for such counselling sessions, and ideally every Tutor should have the use of a 'study' or office – as can be managed by most teachers in boarding schools. Had pastoral care been properly defined in the fifties and its equipment and architectural requirement properly articulated, interview rooms would no doubt have been as much part of the standard spaces of schools as laboratories and libraries. As it is, pastoral care team-leaders are still often without private rooms, and those who have them often had to fight long and hard for them.

However, there are advantages in using the Tutor and the tutor group's own classroom. If the Tutor has managed to make a 'tutor room' of a 'classroom', so that the tutees feel it as their 'homeroom' (the pleasant and useful United States phrase), an 'after-school' talk by the Tutor's desk in *his* room can have an excellent ambience for such a meeting.

Nevertheless, Tutors in a school should seek access to suitable interview/discussion rooms. One way is for an 'interview room' to be set aside for Tutors to book for meetings with parents or guardians and for tutees themselves. One such room can often be found in a school, and even if not adequate, meets some of the need.

Complementing this, or instead of it if such a designated room is not possible, arrangements can be made to use the temporarily vacant offices of head, deputies, or middle-management. This can be awkward, but should not be completely dismissed.

I suggest as a workable routine that a Tutor should have one scheduled interview with each of her tutees in a quiet private comfortable room once a term, with additional opportunities for other occasions as required.

Recording

A frequent fault of all of us in schools involved in helping pupils is over-emphasising our individual contribution and seeing a particular meeting as separate from the longer-term approach. We are therefore often less than punctilious about recording.

A pupil's file should be regarded as a tool of pastoral care: the diagnostic tool to help reflection, analysis, and plans for action. The tutee herself should know of its existence, and its uses. She should sometimes be asked to suggest anything about the term's work and events that ought to go in. The Tutor should ensure that notes on major or minor points are slipped in, however brief they are (provided they are dated!).

I have suggested regular 'review' interviews for tutees. A Tutor will also have interviews with families, the number of which will depend on the devolution within the pastoral aspect of the school. (For instance, some schools have reception or option interviews carried out by middle- or senior-management pastoral responsibility-holders, and others give some of this work to Tutors – a practice I prefer.)

It is essential that a record of every interview is kept if continuity, progress, and the confidence of parents is to be retained. Unless the teacher is able to write up the interview immediately it finishes, which is usually not practicable in a school day, one way is to take very short notes, as unostentatiously as possible, during the interview. It is made easier if one indicates that one is particularly noting the things agreed, especially action to be initiated by the school. Indeed, failure to do so undermines the confidence of the parents and such failures are always referred to in any later interview. The writing-up of the interview needs to be done as soon as possible as, even with outline notes, it is easy to forget what was said – and decided.

121

At the end of the interview there should be an oral summary of any decisions or recommendations and in some cases, a letter should follow stating these clearly in writing.

Colleagues should be kept informed as far as possible, especially with a note of action promised.

The hierarchical team

Schools sometimes find the vertical hierarchy of team leadership very difficult to accept, still more to use effectively. Too easily a mistrust develops, part of the institutional culture of a secondary school, in which the greatest time and the greatest emphasis is properly given to classroom teaching and the relationship of teacher to taught is the one understood best. The result can be that a school is less than clear about when the case of an individual or particular group is referred. Indeed, often disruptive behaviour is regarded as the only trigger for complaint, and methodical consultation and referral is less common.

Ideally you would wish as a Tutor to review the progress of all aspects of the tutees in your care with your team leader in a routine way, say, every half term. These occasions allow you to reflect on each tutee prompted by the senior colleague and thus differently from the daily rush. The apparently less demanding tutee can be focused on: 'What does she need?' 'How is he developing?'

Tutees who are causing concern can be reviewed in terms of the action planned: 'Has the daily report helped her?' 'Is his family making the promised weekly contact?' This is the moment for plans to be changed, so that there is a coherent and continuously applied regime devised for the more worrying cases. (Of course, the middle-management pastoral team leader requires similar reviews, concentrating on the more difficult cases, with the appropriate deputy head.) Such opportunities for reflection, consultation, and planning can convert individual casework from reactive to proactive and give the daily challenges of the next weeks a positive and hopeful coherence. They can also ensure that no one is overlooked because she or he is 'getting along OK'.

Whether or not you have such review sessions in your team, you will need to consult over individual tutees. The criterion for this is not the *seriousness* of the situation, but the need for a second opinion. A major bereavement in a family or an unpleasant incident of racial harassment may be more 'serious' than the boy who is just jogging along, but the action required on the first two may be clear and that on the third baffling. A Tutor always needs to keep his team leader informed, but it is much harder to know when a second opinion is valuable.

It can be difficult to know who is taking responsibility in such cases of collaboration: Are you:

1 merely informing? (For example, Fred's father has come back from abroad.)
2 informing and suggesting simple action supportive to you? (For example, Happy Begum's father has died after a long illness. Would you please send a letter on behalf of the school?)
3 consulting? (For example, Martin is being kept away from school and my notes are getting nowhere. Any ideas?)
4 referring? (For example, I've done all I can to help Leila get herself to school on time. Could you please take over?)

Clarity of responsibility is essential. In the cases of a referral, it is wise to be sure which aspects are being referred, and to have a clear return hand-back. You cannot afford to be unclear which of you is currently taking responsibility for which aspects of care.

The good Tutor is not one who manages to handle everything himself, but one who knows how to use her team leader, consulting, seeking help, and referring sensitively.

External support

Just as the pastoral staff inside a school have to work as a team, the school cannot, and would not wish to aspire to, offer the full range of personal, educational, and vocational support that young people need. Indeed, one of the tutorial skills is to ensure that tutees are put in touch with appropriate specialist agencies, or their support is elicited. Each school will, quite properly, have somewhat different arrangements for referring to outside agencies. It is unusual for Tutors to have this as a first responsibility, though it is occasionally so.

Certainly, however, the Tutor will be expected to be the first point of diagnosis of the possible need to refer and also should thereafter continue as a key figure. What should the Tutor be looking for?

Firstly, a school will want its pupils to have at the least the minimum physical and financial necessities. The Tutor, therefore, will be alert to any signs of acute poverty, inadequate clothing, news of housing difficulties, clues of heating deficiencies. The school will want to be sensitive, to follow up such worries, and seek what help it can. Usually worries of this sort will require consultation with the Education Welfare Service. Sometimes a school will additionally have trust funds available to help. Usually problems in these categories will need to be referred to the middle-management pastoral team leader, but the Tutor is best placed to pick up the clues to the need.

Secondly, the Tutor will keep an eye open, in however a non-specialist way, for apparent health problems. Of course, virtually every pupil comes to secondary school with a medical record and routine medicals follow. However, the lay eye of the Tutor is a necessary complement: are there any unexpected signs about complexion, breathing, eyes, hearing, movements? For instance, hearing difficulties ('glue ear') can go undiagnosed because they are intermittent, but can substantially impede learning. A Tutor will want to be alert to comments from subject teachers, observant, appropriately enquiring, and willing to discuss and refer. Although families are understandably sensitive to suggestions that there is undiagnosed bad health, the Tutor is the most likely professional to be able to notice this when it does occur.

An extreme case of this is child abuse – emotional, physical, or specifically sexual. In recent years sexual abuse has been increasingly recognised, and even the most conservative estimates are much higher than was thought up to, say, the end of the seventies. No Tutor can be sure of recognising this, and the evidence is that very many young people keep their secret uncomfortably but successfully to themselves. Nevertheless, there will be occasions when the Tutor picks up a hint, or, indeed, is specifically taken into the confidence of a pupil.

Much sexual abuse is not revealed in any ostensible signs. Nevertheless, the Tutor sensitive and alert to any aspects of behaviour, remarks, or physical signs is more likely than anyone else to notice key clues. These vary from tense, sensitive, closing-in behaviour on the one hand to undue sexual awareness with younger children on the other.

The Tutor who has established a close, mutually respectful relationship is more likely to receive spoken hints or outright pleas for help. However, Tutors must not feel guilty if abuse is found but nothing has been volunteered. It is very difficult for the abused to talk. Care has to be taken over promises of confidentiality: a Tutor simply can't give a blanket promise. It must be made clear that dangerous and illegal activities may well have to be passed on.

This is another example of how individual casework should relate to the overall tutorial programme. A well-prepared part of a programme allows the abused young person to bring into his consciousness that abusive behaviour which very likely has been suppressed. It also allows the tutee to formulate concepts and to develop language which help objectivise the experience – and this makes it easier for the tutee to talk about it. For instance, 'It's my body' in *LTR* Book 2, p. 120 puts the most frequent assumptions about child sexual abuse against the surveyed facts (see opposite). This is one of the aspects of pastoral care which causes Tutors most distress: it is emotionally and mentally painful for us to think about; it is doubly distressing to consider one of our tutees having experienced such abuse; we worry about our comparative ignorance; we worry about the legal situations – and we know of the huge public controversies that have raged.

The particular tension at the heart of the tutorial role is the fact that most sexual abuse is within the family circle, and the victim is torn between affection and love of the offender and abhorrence, often feeling an unreasonable guilt herself, and dreading the results of revelation.

Clearly the Tutor should not hang on to his doubts or suspicions very long: this is a key instance of the importance of team work. The Tutor's task is not to be an expert in child sexual abuse but an expert on her tutees, noticing signs of fear, sexual provocativeness, being withdrawn, flinching, or just plain misery. The Tutor will hope that the background overall tutorial programme and the mutual trust of Tutor and tutee will permit talk – but the Tutor must not

GETTING TO KNOW YOURSELF

What is the sexual assault of a child?

Sexual assault means **forcing** somebody to be involved in
sexual contact. When you're older, sexual contact will make
you feel close, happily excited, loving, and reassured. Much of
your happiness will come from **choosing** to be close to the
other person, and it will involve feeling that all of your body
and all of your thoughts and feelings are valued. Sexual assault
is different because you're not choosing and how you feel
comes second to the other person's feelings. When children are
the victims of sexual assault, the sexual contact may involve
handling of the child's genitals or the child may be asked to
touch the genitals of the older child or adult. Sometimes the
contact is oral sex, using the child's mouth. Sexual contact can
include trying to be inside the vagina or anus. Other kinds of
assault don't involve any kind of physical contact; a child may
be forced to look at the genitals of the other person or to
undress. Whatever happens, children can't be ready for sexual
contact with another person until they have grown up, and can
choose for themselves what they want to do.
What most people think happens when a child is assaulted
and what really happens are often quite different:

What most people think	What is much more common
A dangerous, weird stranger	A person they know, often a relative or friend of the family, is more often the offender (85% of cases)
Isolated incident	Over and over again
Out of the blue	A situation that develops gradually, over a period of time
Rare and extreme	Frequent incidents. There are many forms of sexual assault
A violent attack	Subtle, rather than extreme force

be disappointed or resentful if the abused tutee cannot share the distress.

The earliest worries should be discussed with the pastoral team leader. I think it is normally not wise initially to share the worries with other colleagues. This is possibly the most highly charged aspect of pastoral care. The pastoral team leader will normally discuss with the Educational Welfare Officer, and the Tutor should always remain part of the team. There is a tendency in a few schools for the major issues to rocket 'to the top', leaving the Tutor floundering! In my view wise pastoral care procedures in schools keep the Tutor as an active part of the team throughout: he has the widest knowledge of the young person, the daily contact, and the continuing responsibility. (For inter-agency co-operation see DHSS, 1988.)

The non-school specialist with whom the Tutor is likely to have most contact is the Education Welfare Officer or Educational Social Worker. We are not at our best working with professionals outside teaching, for we usually have no training and little experience. We tend to underestimate the Education Welfare Officers, at our worst treating them as messengers to take the school's wishes to elusive families. Professional folk memories of 'the School Board man' chasing truants will lurk unarticulated at the back of our minds. We see the Education Welfare Officer as an emissary of the school.

More generally we tend to distrust the 'lack of understanding' of psychologist, social worker, counsellor, and physician, who don't work in schools. Rather than persuade them of our point of view, we should relish theirs. The Education Welfare Officer rightly has a different point of view, speaking for the overall needs of a student as a person and not primarily for the overall needs of the class. Disagreements are inevitable and need not be unhealthy. Indeed, it is dangerous to presume that we all have or should have the same perspective. It is professional to disagree.

Relating to other colleagues

One of the hardest aspects of tutoring is relating to the needs of the tutees on the one hand and the responses of colleagues on the other. A Tutor is likely to find a number of occasions when his personal and professional loyalty is made stressful by allegations from a tutee that a colleague teacher is treating him wrongly or unfairly: 'Miss, that Mr Charles, do you know what he called me?' 'Sir, it doesn't matter what I do in Jones', I mean Mr Jones' class, he always picks on me, just for breathing funny like, the moment I come in the room!'

The traditional camaraderie of the staff has an unspoken principle that an offence against one is an offence against all, and, even more dubiously, that the judge on whether a look, word, or act is an offence is the teacher who has been offended. Some schools have endeavoured to establish whole-school disciplinary codes to avoid the grosser possible variations. This is required by the current conditions of service (DES, 1987, p. 20) and the 1986 Education Act (Section 22). Even with such statements, however, there will be variations between colleagues, and there will certainly be allegations of unfairness by one of your tutees and allegations against them by other colleagues.

No advice will meet all occasions, but some principles can be established. In the first place, don't react too quickly or jump to a conclusion at the first description: things are rarely as they seem. Tutees have to learn that ill-considered complaints will not be taken at face value and criticisms of a teacher cannot be offered as a mere defence in a pre-emptive strike. On the other hand, they must also trust their Tutor to listen and support them when appropriate. A Tutor's professional integrity is thus tested.

There will be occasions when your need is to help your tutee towards a reconciliation when he has been in the wrong. This is the educational heart of tutoring because it enables the tutee to reflect, understand how and why he went wrong, and to devise appropriate ways to apologise and make positive moves forward.

When, though, it is patently clear that the other teacher is wrong the problem is greater. You are responsible for your tutee's behaviour but not for your colleague's. If your tutee is merely misunderstood, a chat with your colleague may allow her to see your tutee in a different light. If there has been a factual misunderstanding, it is not too difficult to put right. However, there might be occasions when your tutee has suffered a definite indignity from unprofessional conduct: a physical punishment, a racist remark, a family jibe. The tutee has a right to look to you for support.

It is on such occasions that your reputation for even-handedness will be subconsciously scrutinised. You may be able to have a friendly, even jocular word, with the colleague concerned. If she concedes, the problem can be readily resolved, and you could attempt a reconciliation by taking your tutee to see the colleague. If, though, there is no offer or concession you have a stark choice between staffroom comfort and professional comfort, but you cannot ignore the situation. If the event is not too serious or hurtful you can counsel the tutee to let it pass on the grounds that some unpleasantness and even injustices are not worth fighting and are best forgiven or forgotten. On the other hand, you may have to face your colleague with the awkward position you are in: you cannot silently overlook the fact that he hit your tutee or she used racist language. If the event was an inadvertent, momentary slip, surely we can find a way of reconciliation. However, if that is unacceptable to the colleague, you are sorry but you simply have to ask someone to take it over.

Such action is the *professional* thing to do: your duty as a Tutor is to ensure your tutees have their entitlement at school, and that includes fairness, protection from violence, and protection from improper personal remarks.

In some ways an even more difficult problem is the more intangible complaints, such as: 'She doesn't do anything with me, Sir!' 'He can't keep us in order, really.' As the Tutor's task is to assist the tutees towards their entitlement, she must be distressed at the suggestion that her tutees are having unsatisfactory subject teaching in whatever way. The tutorial period discussion has to be handled with care: can the tutees express their disquiet courteously and without rancour? Can they be precise without exaggeration? Can they consider what in their behaviour individually or severally may have contributed to or even created the difficulty? Most importantly, can the Tutor Group as a whole find a way of putting its view to that teacher?

It will be seen that, as in so much of tutoring, the reaction to events and the care of the individual has a reciprocal relationship with whole-group tutorial work. Such discussions should be underpinned by the tutorial programme approach to getting on and not getting on with people (cf. Chapter 4, pp. 61–8, and *LTR* Book 1, pp. 78–83). The particular discussion of *this* sequence of events will itself be part of the 'programme', real and immediate 'material' to join the simulated, factual, or fictional of the presented programme. 'What,' asks the Tutor, 'can we do?' If the group admits some culpability, the group can find ways of righting that and apologising. If not, the task of responsibility for the action must lie with the Tutor. The tutees have played their role by sharing their grievance with their

Tutor. If the Tutor cannot decently see it as a mere temporary aberration and help the individual or the group to accept it, she must take it up in confidence with the individual, her team leader, or the Tutor's team leader.

Conclusion

A Tutor, however caring, ambitious, and hardworking, is not ultimately responsible for all aspects of his tutees and must not feel over-burdened: the hierarchical structure must be able to take over. The school's responsibility for the welfare and growth of the individual pupil will be lodged with the Tutor 'in the first instance'. The Tutor's art and craft has two aspects. The first is relating individual casework to whole-group discussion and the tutorial programme, and the second is knowing when to hand over to his or her senior. A Tutor cannot keep a tutee to him- or herself: the school's teamwork is required.

8 The Tutor's style

Introduction

Perhaps more than in any other aspect of teaching, the successful Tutor is one who uses but does not exploit her own personality and personal approaches. There is in all roles in a school a tension, which can be fruitful or destructive, between self and task.

There is clearly a problem of confidentiality: one of the main reasons for locating such a major curriculum responsibility in the tutorial programme under the heads of year or houses is to link the personal and social development aspects of the whole-school curriculum with the very close knowledge of the pupil and his or her family that house or year head and Tutor have. (For instance, a Tutor will have read all the files of her tutees; a subject teacher cannot do all this for every pupil in all her classes, or indeed for any but a handful.) This knowledge makes links between pupil situations and the topic and their material possible and profitable, but it also risks exploiting confidential knowledge in the 'group'. The Tutor will have to guard against this, whilst not wishing to lose or waste the intimacy of her knowledge.

The tutorial environment

Ideally, a whole school community should be characterised by quiet, good organisation that encourages all the teachers to relate warmly though firmly to all students. Schools where a combination of architectural, organisational, student composition, and staffing problems lead to tensions and confrontations will be communities in which it is considerably harder for any teacher to work effectively for the students' personal and social development. Some schools offer an unsympathetic environment. Many, indeed, are harsh physical environments in which wall textures, acoustics, graffiti, and the ugly combine to create a need to shout, be surly, and be tense. Many are visually starved of works of art, pupils' work, interesting displays, signs of the real world, or, indeed, anything on which the eye can light with pleasure. (The Elton report confirms this: see Committee of Enquiry, 1989, pp. 115–18.)

In such schools and in others better placed physically there can be an inter-personal regime that is equally destructive: adults ignore pupils, are abrupt, shout, or are sarcastic. The procedure lacks warmth or dignity. It is of such schools that David Hargreaves has written that:

> Our present secondary school system, largely through the hidden curriculum, exerts on many pupils, particularly but by no means exclusively from the working class, a destruction of their dignity which is so massive and pervasive that few subsequently recover from it.
>
> (Hargreaves, 1982, p. 17)

Instead, the school as a whole should be a warm, celebratory, flourishing community, with pride in itself, the achievements of its members, and the obvious goodwill of all. There needs to be, and can be, a strongly expressed sense of the personal worth of each person. The Tutor, it has to be admitted, can make only a modest contribution to the overall climate of relationships in the school, and the Tutor's own work with the Tutor Group will be made harder if that over-all climate is harsh.

However, within the group, Tutors are well advised to establish a carefully controlled style which is efficient, fair, interested, positive, and warm. From the mutual respect of member to member grows the wider respect for others. Personal and social development is best enhanced in the context of a Tutor Group which is a supportive 'group' and in a tutor room that is a true 'homeroom'. To achieve this within his group, then, each Tutor will want to consider the following:

1 The physical environment

To what extent can you make your room more pleasing, more welcoming, more stimulating? The ingenious Tutor can use pin boards, bookshelves, plants, and pictures to soften a room.

2 A spirit of fairness and caring

If members of the group are to develop as individuals, they must be helped to see that everything is done fairly and that each cares for each. Small touches, like the Tutor's sending messages home about family events, sympathy offered to a boy who has lost something, or the group celebration of an individual's happiness can build up a caring group feeling.

3 Group responsibility

As far as possible the group as a whole should discuss and make joint decisions of all kinds. In this way, also, the group can start to take responsibility for each other − helping the girl who is easily late or the boy who often forgets.

4 Build up a sense of achievement

Whenever possible, bring in work from the visual arts, the tutees' writing, their subject folders, and extra-curricular events, praise them and display them.

Working with uncertainty

Even the most knowledgeable and experienced subject teacher will find occasions when she is uncertain about the full facts, correct explanation, a proper way of presenting some aspect of the syllabus or a topic that arises. However, her teacherly stance is reasonably one of knowing most aspects that the pupil has to cover.

This is not the case for the Tutor. Indeed, even the most knowledgeable and experienced of us will know ourselves to be ignorant of many topics that belong to 'personal and social development'. Even when we have some knowledge, we are likely to be uncertain and know our limits. For instance, the development of understanding of HIV has been so rapid (see Rogers, 1989) that even a group of Health Education experts will disagree about some key details of transmission. Probably no teachers are going to be confidently knowledgeable, and most of us are going to know how little we know. For instance, a secondary-school woman headteacher was asked by girls in the fourth year whether women could pass HIV to other women. She had to say that she did not know. (Indeed, it proves to be less than clear: it is 'biologically plausible' that lesbian lovers could transmit HIV from vaginal fluids through saliva, but no cases have been recorded.) Similar ignorance is the frequent experience of Tutors. It is an inevitable part of full tutoring – as it is of parenting.

Further, it could be argued that lack of knowledge and lack of certainty are not only inevitable but desirable for the Tutor over a range of his work. A subject teacher may reasonably hope to be happily confident over, say, much of the field of geography. But if the Tutor's 'subject' is 'the pupil himself', the Tutor would not pretend to such major knowledge.

Perhaps one could think of the Tutor's knowledge of the tutee and of life as a Venn diagram:

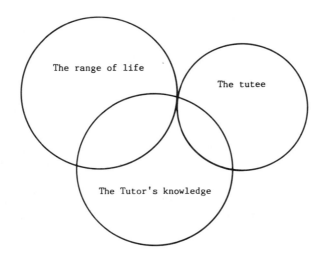

At the intersection of the Tutor's knowledge with the other two circles is tutoring: but that tutoring has to pay respect to the unknown or only slightly known outer segments of the other circles.

Such 'not knowing' is indeed a major mode of tutoring, and the Tutor needs to feel confident with it, sharing uncertainty without being tentative in style.

The personal and the private

In handling many of the aspects of tutorial work Tutors are faced with often difficult and subtle questions of how 'open' or 'personal' to be. On the one hand, the sensitive and conscientious Tutor rightly fears being too 'distant' and 'impersonal', even 'cold', about those many topics which are essentially 'warm', 'personal', and 'delicate'. On the other hand, questions of tact, probity, and reticence lead most of us to worry lest we should lay ourselves open to being hurt (perhaps by receiving mockery), being accused of pushing our own views, or prying into the lives of families. Many aspects of the curriculum involve controversial issues – literature, politics, even the apparent objectivity of the sciences. A school, a teaching team, and each individual teacher has, of course, to develop a policy on the covering of contentious issues. The extended responsibility for the curriculum and management of the school following the 1986 and 1988 legislation sharpens the need for a school to develop a policy. Such a policy both helps and protects individual teachers, whilst enabling them to develop further skills. Only with such an approach can pupils be brought positively to grapple intelligently for themselves with the powerful contentious issues of their lives.

A good start for considering such a policy is this description by David Hargreaves when he was Chief Inspector for the ILEA:

> Good practice therefore must involve the development of objective procedures. It must attempt to detect bias, root out prejudice and examine evidence so that young people have the knowledge or skills between alternative

interpretations or points of view. Such procedures rest upon the values of respect for others, toleration and fairness.
(ILEA, 1986, pp. 9–10)

Too much of the years of secondary schooling are characterised by an emotional starvation. The Tutor will want warmth, lightness, emotion, and fun in the tutor room. She will want an atmosphere in which feelings, hopes, worries, and joys can be shared, but will seek to achieve this without breaking an appropriate privacy.

One of the arts of the Tutor is *to be personal without being private*. Many of the units in the *LTR* books would wither if there were not a 'personal' tone, but the Tutor should not confuse this with either revealing her or his own privacies or intruding into the tutee's. For a teacher to offer inappropriate intimacies about his private domain is in effect a challenge to the tutee's privacy because of the implicit expectation of reciprocation. Conversely, a Tutor who offers details of his private personal life risks not only offending the tutee and her family but also prompting further probes, which can then offend the Tutor.

There is clearly a problem of confidentiality: one of the main reasons for locating such a major curriculum responsibility in the tutorial programme under the heads of year or houses is to link the personal and social development aspects of the whole-school curriculum with the very close knowledge of the pupil and his family that house or year head and Tutor have. This knowledge makes links between pupil situations and the topic and their material possible and profitable, but it also risks exploiting confidential knowledge in the group. The Tutor will have to guard against this, whilst not wishing to lose or waste the intimacy of her knowledge.

Towards good behaviour

There need be no tension between 'care' and 'control'. The disciplinary requirements of any school relate to the pastoral curriculum in such a way as respect for persons grows out of the whole pastoral curriculum, and especially the tutorial programme:

> The thrust of a truly personal and social education, of a school and a curriculum which is truly pastoral, will be to create conditions within which children will move as quickly and painlessly as possible to a position where they understand and cherish the values which the school should exist to promote: rationality, an open mind, a concern for the truth, respect for persons and so on.
>
> (Best, 1988, p. 5)

Michael Rutter stresses the difference between 'house rules' and 'moral values' (Rutter, 1983, pp. 62–3 and 68–9), pointing out that they should not be confused: a school building, like every other community, will have practical regulations. These are to be followed for convenience and order. As he says, 'It is important . . . that we do not create major moral issues where none exist' (ibid.).

Just as we should not elaborate 'house rules' into morality, I do not consider we can demand fully 'adult' ways of behaving from school students. The phrase we sometimes fall back on: 'How can you expect me to treat you as if you were an adult if you behave like that?' surely demonstrates a misunderstanding: the pupil is *not* adult and his 'childness' has to be respected. That is not to suggest that we accept, still less condone, any form of bad behaviour, but that we do not expect to help the child by appealing to a non-existent adulthood.

140

Conversely, however, our professional stance has always to be deliberately adult: our courtesy, sensitivity, vocal tone, humour, and helpfulness are not only a management method, they are themselves a form of teaching.

The Tutor's example

In a slightly different but equally important way the tutees learn from the interactions with their Tutor and her personal ways.

It is a truism of life that example teaches more than exhortation, and parents and teachers have always known that how they are to each other and to young people is an important component of educating young people. Adolescents say this themselves, and a research study of teenagers in this country confirmed that they felt little changed by advice on how to behave if those giving it did not themselves embody that advice in their ways of relating (McPhail et al., 1972).

It is striking how much a Tutor can influence her tutees by the apparent intangibles of personality and her own interpersonal behaviour to other adults as well as to pupils. Michael Rutter helpfully focuses this in the following polarity:

Sometimes we may wish that our children would 'do what we say', rather than 'do what we do' but it is clear that, when they clash, children tend to follow their percepts of our values, rather than our precepts of what they should practise. Children show a marked tendency to 'model' their behaviour on that of those whom they love, trust and respect.

(Rutter, 1983, p. 69)

141

The atmosphere of tutoring

All aspects of teaching offer the problem of how objective or how personal the teacher should aim the discourse and interaction to be. Although there will be cool, even distant, sequences in tutoring, there needs also be warmth, celebration, and joy. An American researcher said after his study of 1000 United States classrooms 'There was remarkably little evidence of joy in learning . . . and the emotional tone was remarkably uniform' (Goodlad, 1984, p. 7).

Whilst the discipline must be exemplary, the organisation meticulous, and the curriculum planning for the tutorial programme rigorous, there has to be another dimension: the tutorial warmth. Of course, 'warmth', perhaps more professionally known as 'empathy', is an element of all successful lessons, and equally certainly the sloppiness that sometimes creeps in of 'pastoral care equals warmth' is incomplete and dangerous, but there is nevertheless a real sense in which a heightened empathy is the essential *core* of pastoral care.

The Tutor will always need to be rigorous in all respects, but without a patent warmth the Tutorial Group and its work will lack heart and conviction. The tension between generous warmth and objective judgement is the stuff of the tutorial atmosphere.

It is out of this feeling that the Tutor will be able to counsel the occasional acceptance of difficulty and even unfairness: 'Yes, Mr Jones treated you unfairly, but sometimes life is just like that. There's really little we can do.'

Conversely, it is out of such a warmth that there comes the flow of positive and generous spirit that encourages tutees to offer their titbits of information: 'He did really well in Art today; he got a commendation, Miss!'

The effective Tutor will bed the work of the group into a warm soil, and out of it will grow trusting activities.

142

Sharing with other Tutors

Generally speaking, tutor teams are, for a variety of reasons, less cohesive and less used to working together than subject departments. In devising aspects of the tutorial programme, in considering how to handle it, in sharing ideas about ways of working with tutees, Tutors are immensely strengthened if they share ideas between themselves.

For instance, in planning the whole-group work, extra material may be desirable. One can devise it for this topic and one for that. More than that, if Tutors in a year come to sections of the tutorial programme in a staggered sequence, reactions, planning, ideas for approach can be shared, based on the experience of the first user.

Ideally, a team should build up 'sub-specialists', each of whom focuses on an aspect of the tutorial programme. Thus, one member might especially consider information-handling skills and study skills, another education in sexuality, and so on. In some cases this could develop virtually as team teaching, or team tutoring!, with some visits from other teachers to certain tutorial sessions, so that strengths are utilised to the fullest.

Overall it is important to do as much as possible to contribute to the tutorial team, to help build up as a complementary team, and to use its strengths. Tutoring can be a lonely business, though many team leaders work hard to avoid this. The Tutor in a real team is stronger than the Tutor alone.

Conclusion

The work of the successful Tutor will enable the students to take rational, morally sound, socially responsible, and personally deepening control over their lives in their culture and society.

The Tutor's sensitivity and skill welds the routine and the special, using mechanical tasks like diary checklists to deepen self-awareness. The whole curriculum is served by and serves the Tutorial Programme. The study of how to understand and influence society appropriately relates to the tutee's growing sense of self and her or his responsibilities. The day is shaped by the tutorial framework and the habit of reflecting on their day becomes a cohering force.

The work of secondary-school tutoring, although the least well-prepared for by initial or in-service training and only recently specifically encouraged by central government, is one of the most rewarding aspects of teaching.

Appendix A

The contractual background

The following extracts from *The School Teachers' Pay and Conditions Document 1987* list the main contractual responsibilities of a headteacher and all other teachers:

PART X – Conditions of employment of school teachers

35. The following duties shall be deemed to be included in the professional duties which a school teacher may be required to perform –

Other activities   (2) (a) promoting the general progress and well-being of individual pupils assigned to him;

(b) providing guidance and advice to pupils on educational and social matters and on their further education and future careers, including information about sources of more expert advice on specific questions; making relevant records and reports;

(c) making records of and reports on the personal and social needs of pupils;

(d) communicating and consulting with the parents of pupils;

(e) communicating and co-operating with persons or bodies outside the school;

(f) participating in meetings arranged for any of the purposes described above;

Assessments and reports

(3) providing or contributing to oral and written assessments, reports and references relating to individual pupils and groups of pupils.

(DES, 1989, pp. 23–4)

PART VIII – Conditions of employment of head teachers

Pupil progress

(10) ensuring that the progress of the pupils of the school is monitored and recorded;

Pastoral care

(11) determining and ensuring the implementation of a policy for the pastoral care of the pupils;

Discipline

(12) determining, in accordance with any written statement of general principles provided for him by the governing body, measures to be taken with a view to promoting, among the pupils, self-discipline and proper regard for authority, encouraging good behaviour on the part of the pupils, securing that the standard of behaviour of the pupils is acceptable and otherwise regulating the conduct of the pupils; making such measures generally known within the school, and ensuring that they are implemented;

(13) ensuring the maintenance of good order and discipline at all times during the school day (including the midday break) when

pupils are present on the school premises and whenever the pupils are engaged in authorised activities, whether on the school premises or elsewhere;

Relations with parents

(14) making arrangements for parents to be given regular information about the school curriculum, the progress of their children and other matters affecting the school, so as to promote common understanding of its aims.

(DES, 1987, pp. 19–20)

Appendix B

Longman Tutorial Resources

Devised to bring the ideas of this book to the Tutor room, *LTR* is a series of six books of tutee material, one for each year. The following are the contents lists for the first three books:

Book 1

New place
Rules
Views about your new school
Tutor
New teachers
New lessons
Homework
Learning
Puzzles
How am I doing?
Tutor Group
New friends
Old friends
Friends in other years
Unfriendly people
Getting heard
Working together

In the limelight
Adults in school
Adults around school
Your community
School and home
Families
Boys and girls
Growing and changing
Food

Book 2

Now you're a second year

What's special about being a second year?
Advice to a first year
Looking back and looking forward
What gets you interested?
What puts you off?
Organise your homework
Homework worries
Listening – who, me?
Listening and responding
But I just don't understand!
Improve your cleverness
'Jump boy, jump!'
Getting on with teachers
But of course I'm easy to get on with!

Friends can help you out

Helping friends
Sharing friends
So you think that you know me?

Best friends
We might be friends – but!
Each other's lives
Being the same
Being different
Boys and girls: any real differences?
Who's stronger?
Making space
Girls and boys: a questionnaire

Living in a family

What is a family?
Sharing
Looking after the others
Being responsible
Changing places
Missing someone
When somebody dies
Feeling close

Getting to know yourself

What else do you know about yourself?
Be yourself – how?
Letting go
Being by yourself
Feeling embarrassed
Feeling angry
Feeling worried
Feeling up and down
Finding your values
Your rights – or mine ...
I have the right
Growing up: changing loves

Talking about feelings
Loving friendships
A new liking/loving
You don't like ...!
It's my body
Trying out for myself
At the end of the second year

Book 3

Look for alternatives

Male or female?
Trying to adjust to changes at home
How important are appearances to you?
Early experiences
Division of labour in the home
Learning about your own attitudes:
    'Ask some questions'
Just friends, or more?

Children and adults

Who's got the power?
Children's rights
You have to make decisions
Parent and child: give and take
My dad: Kate's story
Homework — what do parents think?

Options at school

How do you make choices?
What are your feelings about school?

Which subjects will you choose?
How to find more information
What can influence your future?

In and out of work

Jobs for men or jobs for women?
Money and work
Going back to work
The effects of not having a job
Redundancy notice
Look back to how others have had to survive

You and other people

Keep in touch with people around you
Friends — what do they mean to you?
Friendship depends on give and take
What it means to care
Facilities for the disabled
Sisters and brothers
Help new students to settle in
Schools have rules for a variety of reasons

Grow up confidently

Change in your life
Bodycare
Close relationships
Advice: get help when you need it

Learn from experience

For the first time — achievements and turning points
How to lay out your work

How is your work marked?
Assess the way your work is marked: a questionnaire
What affects your learning?
Groupwork
When your teacher is away
Review the year

Appendix C

The National Association for Pastoral Care in Education, NAPCE

This is a nation-wide and very well-established association supporting the pastoral aspect of all forms of teaching, and particularly helpful to Secondary Tutors and their team leaders. Apart from publishing the practical journal *Pastoral Care in Education* (details on page 156), it has a secretariat and information base at Warwick University, an annual residential conference, and submits evidence on behalf of members to all relevant national bodies (for example, DES, NCC, and various committees). Regional and Local Branches offer a range of meetings and short courses which are of great help to Tutors.

Enquiries about NAPCE can be made to The Secretary, NAPCE, Education Department, University of Warwick, Coventry, CV4 7AL (Tel: 0203 523810).

Recommended reading

The Tutor's year is so demanding and busy that it is unlikely that many will have time for extended study of all that she or he might wish. Indeed this book has been deliberately kept short. Full references to all authors cited are given in the next section. This brief list is of books strongly recommended for Tutors wishing to extend their understanding and knowledge. They have been chosen to cover key aspects of tutoring and its interaction with the whole school.

BUTTON, LESLIE (1987), 'Developmental group work as an approach to personal, social and moral education', in Thacker et al. (1987), pp. 130–43. An excellent discussion of the place of group work in PSE by one of the pioneering theorists.

HALL, GEOFFREY (1989), *Records of Achievement, Issues and Practice*, Kogan Page. The best brief overview of the new procedures, and of special interest for Tutors, though written for all teachers.

LEAKE, ALISON, and ROBOTTOM, JOHN (1988), *Tutorial Topics*, Longman. A clearly organised, lively contribution to tutorial work for lower and middle-school classes. It can be used with the successful BBC TV programme of the same name or entirely on its own. The starting point for each section is one of the themes in the BBC series *Tutorial Topics* (available on video).

MACBETH, ALASTAIR (1989), *Involving Parents*, Heinemann Educational Books. A thoroughly researched exploration of the educational and legislative relationship between schools and parents with many practical suggestions.

MAHER, PETER (ed.) (1987), *Child Abuse, The Educational Perspective*, Basil Blackwell. A collection of studies especially for teachers. This is a particularly balanced coverage of this difficult and painful subject.

Pastoral Care in Education, the quarterly journal of the *National Association of Pastoral Care in Education* publishes original contributions on all aspects of the provision of pastoral care in all kinds of educational settings. The journal is published four times a year, in March, June, September, and December, by Basil Blackwell Ltd, 108 Cowley road, Oxford OX4 1JF, in association with the National Association of Pastoral Care in Education. Membership of NAPCE includes a subscription at members' rate to *Pastoral Care in Education*.

PRING, RICHARD (1984), *Personal and Social Education in the Curriculum*, Hodder and Stoughton. Although not specifically written for Tutors, this is the best overview of 'the pastoral curriculum' in its widest whole-school sense and is of great help for Tutors relating tutorial work to the whole curriculum.

ROGERS, RICK (1989), *HIV and AIDS: What Every Tutor Needs to Know*, Longman Tutorial Resources, Longman. Specifically focused on the needs of Tutors, this is a short, readily comprehensible, and soundly researched booklet. It was written on the advice of medical specialists brought together by the Faculty of Community Medicine and teachers for the membership of the National Association for Pastoral Care in Education.

SCHOOL CURRICULUM DEVELOPMENT COMMITTEE and the NATIONAL ASSOCIATION FOR PASTORAL CARE IN EDUCATION (1989), *Whole Person: Whole School, Bridging the*

Academic/Pastoral Divide, Longman. A helpful brief booklet on the relationship of pastoral care to the remainder of the curriculum.

* * * * * * * *

Bibliography

This is a complete list of all references in the text together with additional books that I have drawn from in writing this book.

ARMSTRONG, DAVID (1985), 'How do we help children learn from their experience in the school organisation?' in Lang, Peter and Marland, Michael (eds), *New Directions in Pastoral Care*, Basil Blackwell.

ARORA, C. M. J. and THOMPSON, D. A. (1987), 'Defining Bullying for a Secondary School', *Education and Child Psychology*, 4, 4, 110–20.

ASHER, S. R. (1978), 'Children's Peer Relations', in Lamb, M. E. (ed.), *Social and Personality Development*, Holt, Rinehart and Winston, pp. 91–113.

BALDING, JOHN (1987), 'Health Education', in Thacker et al., pp. 172–9.

BECHER, T., ERAUT, M. and KNIGHT, J. (1981), *Policies For Educational Accountability*, Heinemann.

BEST, RON (1988), 'Care and Control – are we getting it right?', in *Pastoral Care in Education*, 6, 2, June 1988, 2–9.

BLACKBURN, KEITH (1983), 'The Pastoral Head: A Developing Role', in *Pastoral Care*, vol. 1, no. 2, Feb. 1983, pp. 18–24.

BLACKBURN, KEITH (1983), 'Building a Pastoral Curriculum', in Blackburn, Keith, *Head of House, Head of Year*, Heinemann Educational.

BOTVIN, GILBERT, ENG, ANNA and WILLIAMS, CHRISTINE (1980), 'Preventing the Onset of Cigarette Smoking through Life Skills Training' in *Preventive Medicine*, vol. 9, pp. 135–43, 1980.

BRANDT, GODFREY L. (1986), *The Realisation of Anti-racist Teaching*, Falmer Press.

BRECHT, BERTOLT (1954) *Die Ausnahme und die Regel*, first published in Moscow in 1937. English translation by Eric Bentley, first published as *The Exception and the Rule* in *Chrysalis*, Boston, vol. VII, nos. 11–12, 1954. First UK edition in *Spotlight*, edited by Michael Marland for schools, Blackie, 1966.

BROWN J. M. and ARMSTRONG, R. (1982), 'The Structure of Pupils' Worries During Transition from Junior to Secondary School', *British Educational Journal*, 8, 2, 123–31.

BULMAN, LESLEY and JENKINS, DAVID (1988), *The Pastoral Curriculum*, Basil Blackwell.

BUTTON, LESLIE (1987), 'Developmental group work as an approach to personal social and moral education', in Thacker et al. (1987), pp. 130–43.

CHARLTON, ANNE and BLAIR, VALERIE (1989), 'Absence from school related to children's and parental smoking habits', in *British Medical Journal*, vol. 298, Jan. 1989, pp. 90–2.

COMMISSION FOR RACIAL EQUALITY (1988), *Learning in Terror! A survey of racial harassment in schools and colleges*, CRE.

COMMITTEE OF ENQUIRY, chaired by Lord Elton (1989), *Discipline in Schools*, HMSO.

CONSULTATIVE COMMITTEE ON THE CURRICULUM (being the principal advisory body of the Secretary of State for Scotland on the school curriculum) (1987), *Curriculum Design for the Secondary Stages*, CCC.

COVINGTON, M. B. and BEERY, R. G. (1976), *Self-Worth and School Learning*, New York: Holt, Rinehart and Winston.

COWLEY, JAMES et al. (eds) (1981), *Health Education in Schools*, Harper and Row.

DEL GRECO, LINDA (1980) 'Assertiveness Training for Adolescents: a potentially useful tool in the prevention of cigarette smoking', in *Health Education Journal*, vol. 39, part 3, pp. 80–3.

DEPARTMENT OF EDUCATION AND SCIENCE (1987), *School Teachers' Pay and Conditions Document, 1987*, HMSO.

DEPARTMENT OF EDUCATION AND SCIENCE (n.d., but 1988), *Education Reform*, DES.

DEPARTMENT OF EDUCATION AND SCIENCE (1989), *National Curriculum, From Policy to Practice*, DES.

DEPARTMENT OF HEALTH AND SOCIAL SECURITY AND WELSH OFFICE (1988), *Working Together, A guide to arrangements for inter-agency co-operation for the protection of children from abuse*, HMSO.

DUNCAN, CARLTON (1988), *Pastoral Care: An Antiracist/Multicultural Perspective*, Basil Blackwell.

DWECK, CAROL (1977), 'Learned Helplessness and Negative Evaluation', in *Education*, vol. 19, no. 2, Winter 1977, University of California and Graduate School of Education, pp. 44–9.

EDUCATION (No. 2) ACT 1986 (1986), HMSO.

ERIKSON, ERIK H. (1968 and 1971), *Identity, Youth and Crisis*, Faber.

FRUDE, NEIL and GAULT, HUGH (eds) (1984), *Disruptive Behaviour in Schools*, John Wiley.

GOODLAD, JOHN (1984), *A Place Called School*, McGraw-Hill.

GREEN, JONATHAN (1988), *The Slang Thesaurus*, Penguin. (New edition of 1986 Hamish Hamilton publication.)

HALL, GEOFFREY (1989), *Records of Achievement, Issues and Practice*, Kogan Page.

HAMBLIN, DOUGLAS (1981), *Teaching Study Skills*, Basil Blackwell.

HAMBLIN, DOUGLAS (1986), *A Pastoral Programme*, Basil Blackwell.

HARGREAVES, DAVID (1982), *The Challenge for the Comprehensive School*, Routledge and Kegan Paul.

HARGREAVES, DAVID (1984), *Improving Secondary Schools*, ILEA.

HERBERT, GRAHAM (1989), 'A Whole-Curriculum Approach to Bullying', in Tattum, Delwyn P. and Lane, David A. (eds), *Bullying in Schools*, Trentham Books in association with the Professional Development Centre.

HMI (1982), *The New Teacher in School*, HMSO.

HMI (1987), *Quality in Schools: The Initial Training of Teachers*, HMSO.

HMI (1988), *The New Teacher in School*, HMSO.

HMI (1989), *Personal and Social Education from 5 to 16*, being Curriculum Matters 14, HMSO.

HOBSON, B. and SCALLY, M. (1981), *Life Skills Teaching*, Mc-Graw-Hill.

HURD, DOUGLAS (1988), 'Tamworth Speech', Home Office.

ILEA (various) Research and Statistics, *The Secondary Transfer Project*, Bulletins 1–17.

ILEA (1985), *Westminster City CE SB School, Full Inspection Report*, ILEA.

ILEA (1986), *La Retraite RC High School (SG) Full Inspection Report*, ILEA.

ILEA (1986), *The Teaching of Controversial Issues in School*, ILEA.

IRVING, ANN (1985), *Study and Information Skills Across the Curriculum*, Heinemann Educational Books.

JAYNE, EDITH (1982), *Management Training for Senior Staff, Trained for the job?* (Report No. 2), ILEA Research and Statistics, RS 794/82.

JOHNSON, DAPHNE, et al. (1980), *Secondary Schools and the Welfare Network*, Allen and Unwin.

KELLY, E. and COHN, T. (1988), *Racism in Schools: new research evidence*, Trentham Books.

KIBBLE, DAVID G. (1988), 'Helping Parents through Exams,' in *Pastoral Care in Education*, vol. 6, no. 3, Sept. 1988, pp. 38–41.

KOHLBERG, L. (1982), 'Recent Work in Moral Education', in Ward, L. O. (1982) *The Ethical Dimension of the School Curriculum*, Pineridge Press.

KUTNICK, PETER (1987), 'Autonomy: The Nature of Relationships, Development and the Role of the School', in Thacker et al., pp. 65–77.

LANG, PETER and MARLAND, MICHAEL (1985), *New Directions in Pastoral Care*, Basil Blackwell.

LEAKE, ALISON and ROBOTTOM, JOHN (1988), *Tutorial Topics*, Longman.

MACBETH, ALASTAIR (1981), *The Child Between: a report on School/family relations in the countries of the EEC*, European Commission, HMSO.

MACBETH, ALASTAIR (1989), *Involving Parents*, Heinemann Educational Books.

MCPHAIL, P, UNGOED-THOMAS, J.R. and CHAPMAN, H. (1972) *Moral Education in the Secondary School*, Longman.

MAHER, PETER (ed.) (1987), *Child Abuse, The Educational Perspective*, Basil Blackwell.

MAHER, P. and BEST, R. (1984), *Training and Support for Pastoral Care*, NAPCE.

MARLAND, MICHAEL (1974), *Pastoral Care*, Heinemann Educational Books.

MARLAND, MICHAEL (1980), *Education for the Inner City*, Heinemann Educational Books.

MARLAND, MICHAEL (1981), 'The Pastoral Curriculum', in Best, Ron, et al. (eds), *Perspectives on Pastoral Care*, Heinemann Educational Books.

MARLAND, MICHAEL (1981), *Departmental Management*, edited by Syd Hill, Heinemann Educational Books.

MARLAND, MICHAEL (1981), *Information Skills in the Secondary*

Curriculum, being Schools Council Curriculum Bulletin 9, Methuen Educational for the Schools Council.

MARLAND, MICHAEL (1982), 'Preparing for Promotion in Pastoral Care', in *Pastoral Care*, vol. 1, no. 1, Nov. 1982.

MARLAND, MICHAEL (1983), 'Parenting, School, and Mutual Learning', in *The School and the Family in the European Community*, Commission of the European Community, Luxembourg, 1983; reprinted in Bastiani, John (ed.), *Parents and teachers, 2 From Policy to Practice*, NFER- Nelson, 1988.

MARLAND, MICHAEL (1983), *Sex Differentiation and Schooling*, Heinemann Educational Books.

MARLAND, MICHAEL (1985), 'Parents, Schools, and the Welfare of Pupils', in *Schools and Welfare*, Ribbins, Peter (ed.), Falmer Press.

MARLAND, MICHAEL (1985), *School Management Tasks*, Heinemann Educational Books.

MARLAND, MICHAEL (1986), 'From Headcount to Action: The Analysis of the Progress of the Ethnic Minority Pupils in Schools', in *Multicultural Teaching*, vol. 5, no. 1, Autumn 1986.

MARLAND, MICHAEL (1987), *Multilingual Britain: The Education Challenge*, The Centre for Information on Language Teaching.

MORTIMORE, PETER, SAMMONS, PAM, STORK, LOUISE, LEWIS, DAVID and ECOB, RUSSELL (1988), *School Matters*, Open Books.

NATIONAL ASSOCIATION FOR PASTORAL CARE IN EDUCATION (1986), *Preparing for Pastoral Care, In-Service Training for the Pastoral Aspect of the Teacher's Role*, Basil Blackwell for the National Association of Pastoral Care in Education.

NEWSAM, PETER (1986), 'Racial Prejudice', in *Association for Child Psychology and Psychiatry Newsletter*, vol. 8, no. 1, Jan. 1986, pp. 7–11.

PELLEGRINI, DAVID S. (1985), 'Training in Social Problem-Solving', in Rutter, M. and Hersov, L., *Child and Adolescent Psychiatry*, Blackwell Scientific Publications.

PORTER, RUTH (ed.) (1984) *Child Sexual Abuse within the Family*, Tavistock Publications.

PRING, RICHARD (1984), *Personal and Social Education in the Curriculum*, Hodder and Stoughton.

ROBBINS, L.N. and RUTTER, M. (eds) (1989), *Straight and Devious Pathways from Childhood to Adult Life*, CUP.

ROGERS, RICK (1989), *HIV and AIDS: What Every Tutor Needs to Know*, Longman Tutorial Resources, Longman.

RUDDOCK, JEAN (1983), 'In-Service Courses for Pupils as a Basis for Implementing Curriculum Change', in *British Journal of In-Service Education*, vol. 10, no. 1, Autumn 1983, pp. 32–42.

RUTTER, MICHAEL (1983), *A Measure of Our Values, Goals, and Dilemmas in the Upbringing of Children*, Quaker Home Service.

RUTTER, MICHAEL (1989), 'Pathways from Childhood to Adult Life', in *Journal of Child Psychology and Psychiatry*, vol. 30, no. 1, pp. 23–51, 1989.

RUTTER, MICHAEL, MAUGHAN, BARBARA, MORTIMORE, PETER and OUSTON, JANE (1980), *Fifteen Thousand Hours*, Open Books.

RYDER, J. and CAMPBELL, L. (1988), *Balancing Acts in Personal Social and Health Education: a practical guide for teachers*, Routledge.

STENHOUSE, LAWRENCE (1975), *An Introduction to Curriculum Research and Development*, Heinemann Educational Books.

TATTUM, DELWYN P. and LANE, DAVID, A. (eds) (1989), *Bullying in Schools*, Trentham Books in Association with the Professional Development Centre.

TAYLOR, DEBORAH A. and HARRIS, PAUL L. (1984), 'Knowledge of Strategies for the Expressions of Emotion Among

Normal and Maladjusted Boys: A Research Note', *Journal of Child Psychology and Psychiatry*, vol. 24, no. 1, pp. 141–5.

THACKER, JOHN, PRING, RICHARD and EVANS, DAVID (1987), *Personal Social and Moral Education*, NFER-Nelson.

TIZARD, BARBARA, BLATCHFORD, PETER, BURKE, JESSICA, FARQUHAR, CLARE, and PLEWIS, IAN (1988), *Young Children at School in the Inner City*, Erlbaum.

UNGOED-THOMAS, JASPAR R. (1978), *The Moral Situation of Children*, Macmillan.

WEINREICH-HASTE, HELEN (1983), 'Developmental moral theory, with special reference to Kohlberg', in *Educational Analysis* vol. 5, no. I.

WILSON, JOHN (1972), *Practical Methods of Moral Education*, Heinemann.

Index